10 Keys to Student Empowerment

Discover how to work alongside your students to unlock their potential.

This powerful book reveals 10 keys to creating a classroom where your students can take ownership of their learning and become heroes in their own lives. You'll learn how to build relationships, support, strength, willpower, soft skills, service, agency, curiosity, innovation, and productive failure. Each key is illustrated in a narrative format, designed with tips and notes to help you make practical changes immediately.

By the end of the book, you'll have the foundational pieces you need to create a student-powered classroom where students can learn about themselves, fail forward, and gain courage to face challenges head on.

Cathleen Beachboard (@cathleenbeachbd) has served as an instructional coach, professional developer, and speaker. She currently serves as the Lead Mentor and English Department head for her school, and was the Region Four representative for Virginia modeling the Strategic Instructional Model.

Marynn Dause (@DauseClause) is a National Board-certified teacher with eight years' experience teaching English Language Arts and related topics. She serves as President Elect of the Virginia Association of Teachers of English; prior to that she served five years on the advisory board for the Virginia Student Councils' Association.

Also Available from Routledge
Eye on Education
(www.routledge.com/k-12)

Working Hard, Working Happy: Cultivating a Culture of Effort and Joy in the Classroom
Rita Platt

Passionate Learners: How to Engage and Empower Your Students
Pernille Ripp

Passionate Readers: The Art of Reaching and Engaging Every Child
Pernille Ripp

The Genius Hour Guidebook: Fostering Passion, Wonder, and Inquiry in the Classroom
Denise Krebs and Gallit Zvi

Authentic Project Based Learning in Grades 4–8
Standards-Based Strategies and Scaffolding for Success
Dayna Laur

Authentic Project Based Learning in Grades 9–12
Standards-Based Strategies and Scaffolding for Success
Dayna Laur

Motivating Struggling Learners: 10 Ways to Build Student Success
Barbara R. Blackburn

10 Keys to Student Empowerment

Unlocking the Hero in Each Child

Cathleen Beachboard and Marynn Dause

First published 2020
by Routledge
52 Vanderbilt Avenue, New York, NY 10017

and by Routledge
2 Park Square, Milton Park, Abingdon, Oxon, OX14 4RN

Routledge is an imprint of the Taylor & Francis Group, an informa business

© 2020 Taylor & Francis

The right of Cathleen Beachboard and Marynn Dause to be identified as authors of this work has been asserted by them in accordance with Sections 77 and 78 of the Copyright, Designs and Patents Act 1988.

All rights reserved. No part of this book may be reprinted or reproduced or utilized in any form or by any electronic, mechanical, or other means, now known or hereafter invented, including photocopying and recording, or in any information storage or retrieval system, without permission in writing from the publishers.

Trademark notice: Product or corporate names may be trademarks or registered trademarks, and are used only for identification and explanation without intent to infringe.

Library of Congress Cataloging-in-Publication Data
A catalog record for this title has been requested

ISBN: 978-0-367-18920-4 (hbk)
ISBN: 978-0-367-18922-8 (pbk)
ISBN: 978-0-429-19921-9 (ebk)

Typeset in Palatino
by Swales & Willis, Exeter, Devon, UK

To all of us who have accidentally been called "mom" or "dad" and who eat lunch in two minutes to spend more time with students.
C.B.

To you, friend. If you're reading, this book is for you.
M.D.

Contents

Meet the Authors viii
Preface: Why Unlock Heroes? x
Acknowledgments xii

Key One: Relationships 1

Key Two: Support 15

Key Three: Strength 26

Key Four: Willpower 36

Key Five: Soft Skills 49

Key Six: Service 67

Key Seven: Agency 79

Key Eight: Curiosity 93

Key Nine: Innovation 103

Key Ten: Failure 115

Afterword: Hope 128

Meet the Authors

Cathleen Beachboard has worked for over a decade teaching and empowering students in her English Language Arts classes. Growing up as a struggling dyslexic student, she learned the power of showing people their strengths instead of their weaknesses. Through an amazing student-driven transformation (featured in this book), Cathleen learned the keys to empowerment. Her new life mission is to equip educators and students with the power and the ability to change the world.

Cathleen graduated from West Liberty University with a degree in English Education. Over the years, Cathleen has served as an instructional coach, SIM professional developer, speaker, storyteller, and currently serves as an eighth-grade English teacher at Taylor Middle School.

Cathleen is married to Matthew and together they have seven beautiful children, five of whom they adopted out of foster care during their first year of marriage. Between the kids, their pug, and labradoodle, they have a full house! Cathleen teaches in Fauquier and can frequently be seen on Twitter as @CathleenBeachbd creating digital communities of educational empowerment. She currently moderates the #UnlockingHeroes Twitter chat, a community of educators seeking to support each other and empower students.

Marynn Dause is a National Board-certified teacher who seeks passion and purpose with all of her English Language Arts students. As a trauma survivor and adoptive mother of a teenaged son, Marynn deeply values the social-emotional aspects of education and champions trauma-informed care for all learners. Marynn's goal is to help her students live well by becoming "heroes in their own lives."

Marynn Dause graduated with her B.A. and M.A.Ed. from the College of William and Mary. Marynn serves as President Elect of the Virginia Association of Teachers of English; prior to that she served five years on the advisory board for the Virginia Student Councils' Association. Marynn has taught secondary students in Virginia for eight years. She has also worked as a professional developer, inspirational speaker, tutor, and performance artist.

Preface
Why Unlock Heroes?

Bronnie Ware worked as a palliative carer in Australia. She spent years befriending patients who "had gone home to die." Eventually, those conversations led Bronnie to write an article and a book. She found that the first and most common regret shared by people who were dying was this:

> I wish I'd had the courage to live a life true to myself, not the life others expected of me.
> Bronnie Ware, *The Top 5 Regrets of the Dying* (Hay House)

We're fascinated by Mrs. Ware's quote because death is the great equalizer. It can happen at any time. We're going to die! Maybe tomorrow! And so are our kids. None of us have time to mess around. Sure, we need to teach students to work problems—that's a critical life skill. But scores and grades? Not important. This most common regret of the dying should be a wake-up call to educators. We need to look at children this way: they may die wishing they could have lived better. Look at the people growing before our eyes. Who will they be? How can we fit mathematical thinking into the lives of those folks? How can we fit English and science into these students' stories? That's our purpose. That's why we're here.

In our experience, public education too often feels like a cruise ship. Students are the cargo, or maybe third-class passengers. "We're taking you to be informed, contributing citizens!" teachers shout cheerfully from the bridge. "Sit tight, we'll be there in a jiffy!" Passengers and cargo aren't allowed any part in the working of a ship; they're just along for the ride. No wonder some of ours want to jump off! After all, who wants to stay on a ship whose destination they didn't choose? Then suddenly, the ride is over. Graduation looms, and we release into the world young people who've never learned to sail. Many flounder.

In this way, future generations learn to look to others for direction; they live and die with regret. But there's another way. Students don't have to be "dead weight"—mere luggage in the cargo hold of HMS *Education*. They can be deckhands. Kids can and should learn how to chart destinations. With our help, they can steer through waves. Working together, student sailors can help us adults solve problems. After all, some day they will have to take charge. Students live with fewer regrets when they learn how to pilot ships on their own.

Unlocking Heroes was born when two teachers came to this realization independently. Then, thanks to the magic of algorithms, we connected over Twitter. We were both teachers interested in engaging students with authentic audiences. Flipgrid came into play. The more our students took up leadership roles, the better everyone's learning became. We gave students ownership over goals. Lo and behold, creative, innovative problem solvers formed right before our eyes. Independence gave our kids courage. It was wonderful; eyes sparkled, ideas blossomed, and life in our classrooms took on a new sense of purpose. What was more, we started sharing our own stories of discovery with one another. "Wait, you guys did *what?!*" one or the other of us would gasp. "That's *incredible!*" Worn down as we were at the end of the school year, finding that spark of inspiration in one another was wonderful. It felt a lot like a calm day after storms at sea. We'd like to share that with you, dear reader.

As educators, we're often heavily burdened. Standards, testing, and learning curves occupy our minds. Sometimes, we try hard to keep students quiet and working steadily. Other times, we sacrifice ourselves on the altar of "awesome" in an attempt to engage kids with our very best work. There are good days as well as inevitable bad ones. We've been there; both of us have been guilty of working way too much for insufficient reward. Eventually, we both took a risk; independent of one another, we began experimenting with our pedagogy. We didn't know it at the time, but what we were looking for was "a life true to myself." In the process, we found our way towards real, deep learning. It was frequently messy. There were loud noises and major screw-ups. Sometimes kids got lost in the woods while looking for poetry illustrations … literally.

We hope that by sharing trials and errors from real classes, we can showcase what happens when kids become teachers' co-workers instead of cargo. When students gain the courage to truly *live*, well, that's heroic. By unlocking the heroes within students, we stand to change the course of education forever. Take heart, reader: you are already part of the change. Cathleen likes to say the greatest change comes in "cans": *I **can** read this book, I **can** change my classroom*, and *I **can** change the world*. Keep going. Remember, you, too, were born to be a hero.

Acknowledgments

I (Marynn) would like to acknowledge:

1. The folks who made funny faces when they heard we were writing a book, without whom I couldn't have finished the manuscript.
2. The cashier-baristas at every coffee shop who made funky drinks, no matter how odd, without whom I would have suffered.
3. The students who begged to read the rough draft, only to drop it when they realized it wasn't fiction. You made sure I was on the right path.
4. The friends and family who assured me this was an "awesome" way to spend every weekend. You made sure I kept smiling.
5. Stephensky, X-man, Mater Potater, Emily Dickinson, Taylor Mali, and Stephen again (twice for good measure). For the love.

P.S. Cathleen is the best co-author of all time, and Lauren is the most positive of editors. Cheers to you, ladies!

I (Cathleen) would like to acknowledge:

1. Jeff Zoul, who took a chance when two educators approached him randomly at a professional development to share their vision.
2. Sean Gaillard, Meredith Johnson, Meta Lasch, Nick Napolitano, TMS staff, The Harwell's, Prashant Shrestha, Carol and Ron Beachboard (Mom and Dad), and Evan Carmichael who gave me courage to pursue my story.
3. Phil Strunk, who gave me a model to set up a Twitter community for empowerment.
4. My students. You are the reason for my courage, breakdown, and new beginning.
5. My family. Mom, Matt, my kids CJ, Xander, Dominick, Sydney, Bella, Jacqueline, and Joseph, and my newest family member Marynn: once you write a book together, you're family!

And to all the instigators.

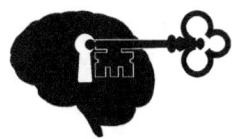

Key One: Relationships

Jensen Armstrong—Student
Loud, opinionated, sarcastic, logophile
Hero

I remember waking up at 5am on a Saturday. I thought, "Maybe this will be fun. Maybe it will be worth it?" Months before, I'd told Mrs. Beachboard that I wanted to get fit for field hockey tryouts. I didn't expect her to offer to train together. Who does personal training with their English teacher? Our end goal was running a 5K— a first for us both. Mrs. Beachboard always insisted that dreams were just goals waiting to be acted on. That's why I was awake so early on a weekend.

We drove to Sheetz to fuel up and have breakfast. Once we finished, we hit the road. We had time, so we talked about everything. It's funny how weeks of training side by side had led up to this pivotal moment. Mrs. Beachboard would run to celebrate her year-long fitness journey; I'd try to set a personal record for speed and endurance.

We arrived at the Bubble Run registration desk. Bubbles were everywhere! An announcement indicated that our wave of runners was up to start. We lined up. Then with a bang! we were off, breathing in unison. The soles of our sneakers made a sort of rhythmic music hitting the pavement. We strived to keep an even pace. As the race progressed, I could see my teacher getting tired. But she was here by my side, pushing me, so I kept running. I wanted to push her back so we could both make it to the end.

Obstacles started to slow us down. This was a bubble run; the bubbles started out fun, but they progressively got more intimidating. Eventually walls of bubbles 10 feet high and three feet thick stood in front of us. We ran into each other. Soap got in our eyes. There were times I debated quitting, but with Mrs. Beachboard by my side I couldn't stop. The race wasn't about me—it was about both of us working together.

Finally, we finished. We'd accomplished what seemed impossible. I knew I was beyond fit for JV tryouts, and Mrs. Beachboard accomplished her goal of ending her weight loss year strong.

In middle school people judge you, and everyone seems to change. Through this race, I learned that people need people. We exist to push each other forward. I was able to help push Mrs. Beachboard, and she in turn helped me. She helped me realize I can always get better. I suppose it wasn't the race that was important, but the moment I realized that I had an impact. I mattered. I learned that I was enough and that it was ok to keep being me, just a better, more bubbly version. I'm still opinionated and sarcastic, but I'm the hero of my own life.

It was an early Tuesday morning, and one of my (Cathleen's) students was lingering after class. He was sort of pacing and asked me if I had a minute. I stopped what I was doing and sat to listen. Nervously, he put his hands together and proceeded to tell me that he loved my class. Needless to say, this was a nice teacher ego boost, and hearing him say it brought a smile to my face. He then proceeded to tell me that he learned in health class that it was unhealthy to be overweight and that he didn't want me to die. Here was one of my favorite students, who I had a great relationship with, telling me I was fat! (To his credit, I was around 285 pounds when he told me this.)

My initial reaction was to be offended, but as I looked past the statement and to his face, I saw caring and compassion. I asked him what he thought I should do. He smiled and prompted me to sit. I sat and listened to his plan for me to set goals and chart progress, to learn in front of my students, and to risk failure for all the world to see. "Hesitant" did not begin to describe the fear I felt. He was giving me an idea because he wanted me to put trust in him and his plan.

For the first time, I let students take over. I was their project, and the goal was helping their teacher. The class was passionate about helping me to succeed. They saw me set health goals, they saw me try, and they saw me research and push myself. As I was risking it all and getting help from my class, something magical started to happen: the students started to set educational goals for themselves and started trying new things. One of my students said, "If you can stop eating Twinkies and bread, then I guess

Figure 1.1 Me (Cathleen) with students at the National School Scrabble tournament.

I can learn to really use a comma." I started learning *with* my students and responded to their suggestions. For the first time, I started listening and reacting to kids' feedback. They felt empowered, and I started to see a world of possibilities through their eyes. Eighteen months later, I'd lost 120 pounds and gained a whole new perspective on student potential. My students were my heroes.

I've heard it said that teachers should be "lifelong learners." Until that moment with my student, I had missed the meaning. I thought that lifelong learning meant professional development classes. Maybe starting a new hobby. But here's the real meaning: true power comes from learning alongside students, not away from them. When I committed to tackling a goal with support from my students, they saw me learn. They knew I trusted them. It helped them begin to trust themselves more, too. Everyone started to get better and push themselves further.

Vulnerability and Heroic Love

Prior to this experience, I had always been the "expert" in the room. I brought in polished, finished lesson plans and activities: from the students' perspective, it appeared that I had no problems (or at the very least, I wasn't going to talk about them). They might be "struggling learners," but I was the hero, the one who had it all figured out … until I started trying to lose weight. Suddenly, my kids saw me authentically struggle almost every day. They witnessed the power of collaboration when I asked them for help and encouragement. I was vulnerable. They saw that I wasn't perfect, and it was ok; on the other hand, students also saw me striving to become better. I knew they loved me because of how they stuck with me when things were hard. They knew I loved them because we were working on something real and personal *together*. That was when it struck me: love. Some kids have it. Some kids don't. All kids *need it*. Love is the first key to unlocking heroes in the classroom, but not that namby-pamby, warm-fuzzies "love" that we so often hear about. Heroic love looks different. Heroic love is loving the unlovable, trusting that kids can truly do anything, and having faith that a child's future is worth every sacrifice.

In those days, I was unaware that there was something keeping me from loving my students as heroes in their own right. It was a monster lurking in classrooms, hallways, and the gymnasium. I held a dangerous, harmful ideal: "perfect." A kid gets a 100? Perfect. A teacher gets 100% pass rate on a standardized test? Perfect. A kid pitched a no hitter? Perfect. The school wins first prize? Perfect. Perfect is awesome—perfect should be rewarded. But in reality?

> A kid battles waking up every day since the funeral of his mother.
> Real.
> A teenager gets hundreds on everything but struggles to find friends.
> Real.
> A child has great siblings and comes from a good home but acts aggressive.
> Real.

Figure 1.2 Finisher photo after Jensen (a student from the class I was teaching) and I (Cathleen) finished the 5K Bubble Run in June 2018.

Ready for a cliché? Actual perfection doesn't exist. However, nobody likes to be told what to do. ("Don't push the big red button? *I'm gonna push it!*") Since people know perfection isn't possible, what do we do? We force reality. We try to get every child to "succeed"—aka to be perfect at school. But here's the thing: when we idolize perfection, we lose our ability to form loving relationships with students. Reality is imperfect, so real love can only exist in that space. By shutting my students out from my problem solving and creating, I unintentionally set up a classroom where perfection was both the goal and the norm. I was the super expert. It created off-balanced relationships from the start. In a world of perfection, there is no need for heroes.

Most people we know want to be the hero in their own lives. We want to be world changers, monster slayers (or tamers), and people who are cheered for conquering life's challenges. Kids are no different. But here's the thing: students can't really be *real* about the dragons they're fighting unless we take the lead by doing it first. We don't want students to "fake it 'til they make it." We want them to see that it's ok to fail because real learning is messy. Trust is formed when someone loves you enough to risk being weak in front of you. Our students taught us that vulnerability mattered to them. They saw right through rehearsed "think alouds." When we faked vulnerability, our kids saw that it was ok to fake learning. When we admitted mistakes in the middle of real learning, it resulted in them being willing to take risks and learn from "fails." In our classrooms, "fail" is a verb—active and changeable, just like our students. It's important that we not allow the noun "failure" to sit like a tombstone on our ability to keep trying.

Having the courage to learn and fail with students is one thing, but having the courage to go outside of classroom norms and trust your students to go along with you is another form of teacher vulnerability—which leads us to Marynn's moment of epiphany. She discovered the benefit of imperfection on a day she lovingly refers to as "that tree incident."

Creating Opportunities and Student Leadership

It was my (Marynn's) first year of teaching. As frequently happens, especially to first-year teachers, I was having trouble engaging my 11th-grade students in the prescribed curriculum content. One class in particular couldn't quite see the point of English class beyond preparing for the state-mandated standardized test, which was a graduation requirement.

Since testing time had already come and gone, the students in this class were, to put it mildly, lacking motivation. To make matters worse, the next unit on my teaching calendar for this class in American literature was Transcendentalist Poetry. How in the *world* am I going to get these guys to care and learn this?! I worried, tossing and turning in bed the night before introducing the unit. Then inspiration struck. Thoreau went out to live in the woods for a year when he was writing *Walden*—what if *we* go into the woods, too? The idea was fairly simple: take the students on a walk to the wooded area at the edge of the high school, maybe show them how to build a basic lean-to using branches and leaves, generally get the wiggles out, and then head back to class to read a few pages of transcendentalist literature. It was easy, content-aligned, kinesthetic, and brief: the perfect introductory exercise.

Of course, things began to fall apart almost immediately. Upon leading my students outside, I realized I'd worn the wrong shoes for such an adventure—heels, long skirts, and thorn bushes don't mix well. To make matters worse, the young ladies in the class began complaining almost immediately about their own attire. It seemed like half of the boys were shouting at the girls to quit their "yapping," and the other half were loudly asking "just what in the sam hill are we doing out here, anyway?"

At a loss but determined to see the experiment through, I called my students to gather around me: "We're out here because the next author we're reading went out to live by himself in the woods for a year, and he was a city boy. I wanted to show you guys what it might have been like for him. Girls, I understand you're not really wearing good shoes for hiking in the woods. *holds up foot* I'm not, either. So you and I will stay near this edge where there's grass, and I'll show you how to *thinks quickly* set up a basic campsite using stones and sticks and stuff. Guys, how many of you know how to build a lean-to or fort to go with our campsite?" Here I held my breath. I'd planned to lead the entire exercise myself, but with the girls flatly refusing to participate the way I'd hoped, I was stuck with no way to directly supervise the class in two places at once. There were more boys wearing jeans and boots than there were girls wearing flats and skirts—who would keep the guys in order while I was showing the girls how to build a camp? The ring of trees and open hillsides that had seemed so welcoming and safe in my dreams the night before suddenly loomed large and unwalled. "These kids could go anywhere right now, and there's nothing I could do to stop them."

After a beat where no one said anything, a young man stepped forward from the back of the small crowd of students. "I know how to build a fort, Mrs. Dause," he said. I was surprised; this kid, dressed head to toe in camouflage, was frequently the cause of my daily headaches due to his outspoken dislike of English, school, and civilization in general. Other than to complain, he rarely spoke, and I found myself mildly embarrassed not to have noticed his love for the outdoors before that very moment. I gulped. "Wasn't this kid in the principal's office just last week? Oh God, please don't let me get fired over this."

"Ok, Caleb. Why don't you take a few of the guys to gather materials and build us a nice lean-to?" As I spoke, Caleb's face lit up. He seemed to stand a bit straighter, too. On impulse, I added, "And make it a good one! I want this sucker to fit at least three people and to be completely rain-proof." High expectations, right?

"We're on it, Mrs. Dause," Caleb responded without a trace of his usual sass. "Just leave it to me. Come on, boys." And with that, Caleb, Jacob, Jonathan, and eventually the entire group of 15 or more boys went sprinting into the woods.

Utterly convinced that I'd just watched most of my class run away for good, I turned back to the remaining group of girls and two boys—so called "sneaker heads" who couldn't bear to dirty their newly purchased shoes. "Umm, Mrs. Dause?" one of the girls tilted her head. "Did they just leave? Like are they at Sheetz now or something?" Ignoring the anxiety screaming in my head, I smiled calmly, answered that the boys would be back soon, and got the group to start collecting stones for a "fire ring," leaves for "bedding," and other homemade campsite accoutrements, all the while straining for any sign of the return of Caleb and his impromptu team.

After some time had passed (I can't remember how long it was—I hadn't yet learned to wear a watch to school, and worry made the time feel interminable), the sound of leaves crunching could be heard. Back came Caleb and all the rest, sweating and laughing, as they hauled tree limbs and handfuls of wild grape vines back to "camp." Working swiftly, the boys began assembling a two-sided lean-to. I watched in amazement as Caleb and another similarly uninterested student directed the work. "Move that piece over there, man. Yeah, that's it. Hey, that one'll make a better roof piece. Where's our central pole, anyway?" But something had caught my eye. Trying not to draw undue attention, I walked quietly over.

"This looks great, Caleb," I said, "But, um ... where's Mike?" Michael was a special needs student, a boy with a booming laugh and complex needs in the classroom. "He ran off with you guys, and he's not back here now. I need to know where he is, Caleb."

Caleb glanced at me. "He's coming, Mrs. Dause. Give him a minute." And so he was. Seconds later, Michael emerged from the woods. He was hauling an entire pine tree, the branches broken off to form a roughly hewn log at least twice his own height in length. Panting and heaving, Michael gave me a huge smile and a thumbs up. "He was the strongest one out there, so he volunteered to drag the center pole," Caleb explained. "Nice work, Mike! Come on, guys, get this thing up in the middle so we can finish building."

When it was done, the campsite we'd built in the woods was easily suitable for at least a night or two of sleeping under the stars. And yes, my students returned to our classroom ready to read (and actually absorb!) the beauty of *Walden Pond*. It was one of our most successful units that semester. More important, though, were the relationships that had been built. Mike was everyone's hero for having dragged such a massive piece of wood all by himself; he received high fives and praise on the way back to the classroom, and was the butt of far fewer jokes from then on. Caleb returned to his seat in the farthest corner, but he didn't complain quite as often, and when I asked him for help with classroom chores or errands (which I began doing much more frequently), he nearly always pitched in. As a whole, the class became a happier place.

Trusting in Kids' Ability to Do Good

Through this experience, I began to discover the same things Cathleen had learned while allowing her students to join and even help direct her weight loss journey: trust is powerful. I had to give up leadership in the lesson and was vulnerable in my need for help completing the campsite. My students had to take on leadership roles because I couldn't do everything.

> **Tip for Teacher Heroes**
>
> Know your kids. I knew going in to "tree day" that although my students were bored in the classroom, none of them were malicious or determined to "watch the world burn"—I was fairly confident that they'd go with me on a new experience if I offered it. If you don't know that about your kiddos, *proceed with caution*. Build challenges and take risks with scaffolding and structure so that you can rein things in as needed. Pause and reflect before trying again. It's ok if things don't go as planned. Making the effort to trust students in small ways is still worthwhile!

Imagine if we created lessons where we planned on needing a hero ... where without the students, the lesson would fail. Risky? Yes. Worth it? *Yes!* Building relationships by allowing students to do the good they've said they will do opens doors to opportunities previously unimagined.

Students are usually told to sit still, listen, and complete boring tasks; they can't possibly show us who they really are (in Caleb's case, a natural-born leader of woodsmen) in an environment that's designed for uniformity. Students want to do cool, heroic stuff—they want to make memories and learn through living. Given the opportunity for agency, the vast majority of our students will exceed our plans for them. Like the heroes they are, kids will most often do right—especially if we teach them how.

The end result is students who are more engaged, more alive, and more willing to take risks in the classroom.

Remember ... Heroic Love Can Be Hard

We want to put something out there, though. People are not always likeable. "Relationship building" gets said so frequently that it can sound easy, but it sometimes sucks. Maybe you've seen a cute quote like this:

> "The kids who need the most love
>   will ask for it in the most unloving ways."

However, it will not become real until you are facing a student who is asking for love in a hard way. These kids are often described as "behavior issues" or "frequent fliers." They can be mean, bitter, angry, dismissive, disrespectful, and anything else you can think of to push people away. Their actions don't feel like requests for love—they usually feel like punishable offenses. We are not in any way suggesting that misbehavior shouldn't result in logical consequences; far from it! What we are saying is that all behavior serves a purpose. When students push us or our planned activities away, there's a reason for that action, and sometimes in those moments relationship building needs to take the front seat, as counterintuitive as it sounds.

For example, I (Cathleen) had a student at the start of the year sit at a table with her head down while other students were actively engaged. I proceeded to ask her what she was doing, and she said "nothing." I took the time to do something I've learned to value in relationship building: when kids need love, I love them harder. Doing something totally unprecedented, I asked this girl what she wanted to be when she grew up. She responded that she wanted to be a designer. Since the day's lesson involved doing research, I asked her to research a new design for my classroom's layout. Because we'd already discussed this as a class, she knew I was planning to redesign my room and thus might actually use her ideas. With this real, trusting approach to the activity, she dove into the lesson. What could have become an escalated argument turned into engagement because I'd taken the time to listen and value what she had to say. That student's "head-down, off-task" behavior was serving the purpose of telling me that the assignment did not meet her need for mental stimulation and a valuable purpose for working.

That's true! I (Marynn) could tell a lot of stories along the same lines. Anyone who's been in the classroom more than a few days is likely to have run across students who act out because they crave attention. Most of us have met kids who are distracted and drowsy because they're hungry or haven't slept. Kids can "check out" both because they're being pushed too hard and not pushed hard enough. There's a reason that classroom management is priority #1 when you're learning to teach!

I'm remembering two kids I'll call Troy and Sheila. Their misbehaviors were different—Troy called out in class to make fun of his classmates and Sheila was all but glued to her phone—but both refused to do work for my class. Redirection didn't affect them. Neither did phone calls home or administrative intervention. Troy and Sheila stand out because they were two of the first kids I had the guts to just talk to.

It took some finagling, but eventually I was able to pull them both aside for individual mini conversations. Guess what? Troy wanted to become a teacher. He actually liked school, especially Social Studies and Science, but he was angry at his mother and had decided to fail classes to make her mad at him in return, "So we can fight it out for real." Sheila was distracted and glued to her phone because she'd lost her house to a fire two weeks into the semester; the only belongings she'd been able to save from the flames were her phone and the clothes on her back because she'd had to run with her brother from the living room as the ceiling caught fire above their heads. Sheila wanted desperately to pass my class and to move into "honors" classes because she felt emotionally safer among more academically advanced kids, but every day she reimagined the sounds and smell of fire. Texting with friends and family was the only thing keeping her reasonably sane.

Do you see the pattern? Both Troy and Sheila wanted to be the heroes in their own stories. In fact, they were working hard (albeit in the wrong direction, in Troy's case) at achieving that goal by beating monsters and claiming treasures. Once I'd invited them to share those stories with me, both kids became more willing to trust me. I was able to help them on their journeys; Troy made up with his mom towards the end of the semester, and against all odds, Sheila ended up earning a passing grade.

Learn Their Story

The reason we point out these stories is that when students need more love, they tend to start off by trusting adults less. If you want to unlock students' inner heroes, you have to start by loving them through their imperfections and getting to truly know them. There's never going to be a recipe for trust and relationships; we as teachers will always have to adapt based on individual needs. Mike, for example, could not have led his peers on their mission to retrieve sticks from the woods because it simply wasn't his gift or talent in that situation; he had to be a follower. Sheila would not have been able to lead a classroom exercise in close reading, at least at the beginning of the year. Marynn had to love her through the hard place and listen to her needs and abilities before she could unlock her inner hero.

It will not always be easy, but when you look past a student's initial action to its source, it makes it easier to love him or her in that imperfect moment.

Unlocking Relationships: Big Ideas

Locks:	Keys:
Every kid has a story and I don't have time to learn all of them!	Learn their stories. In the end the time you take learning their stories will help save you time with discipline, figuring out how to reach them, and helping them learn.
Perfection is best.	Be real and be vulnerable.
Content is more vital than caring.	Every kid wants to be valued and cared for. They won't learn your content if you don't care. Give heroic love daily.
Trust is not one of my top priorities.	In order to get trust you have to give it. Every kid wants the chance to be a hero and it starts with trusting the good in your students.

So what? Students are not born heroes—they take on the role through the relationships we create with them.

Quick Resources for Relationships

1. **In a Million Words or Less**
   This "homework" lets teachers get a jump on learning student backgrounds. At the start of the school year, send a request out to students' families. Make sure to set a deadline! Let families know it's critical for you to start building relationships in your classroom.

Here is an example of what the prompt might look like:

In a Million Words or Less

Yes, you are getting a homework assignment! No one knows your child the way you do. As a teacher, it takes me a great deal of time to get to know each student. For this assignment, please use a million words or less to tell me what you think I should know about your scholar. You may write, draw, or create whatever you wish! Feel free to answer questions like: What does your child like? Dislike? What are your child's strengths? Weaknesses? I will read every one, and I will not share your comments with any other person. Take your time, but there is a deadline. Please get "In a Million Words or Less" to me no later than _____.

2. **Pair-Share**

   A quick way to build classroom community is to do a pair-share activity. Write five to ten questions on the board, and have students partner up. Let students know they will use some of what they learn from this activity to introduce their partners to the rest of the class. Students take 30-second turns answering questions until finished; after that, any method of sharing that is quick and lively will work well to let students share what they've learned about one another. This is a great activity to build classroom relationships.

Sample questions might include:

1. What is your first memory of being really excited?
2. What are you good at?
3. What makes you happy?
4. Tell me about your family and what makes them special to you.
5. What is a dream you have?

Further resources: visit our website at www.unlockingheroes.com or use the QR code below:

Reflection on Relationships

A page for you to reflect and write your own thoughts on relationships. Have a great idea or insight? Feel free to share at www.unlockingheroes.com

_____
_____
_____
_____
_____
_____
_____
_____
_____
_____
_____
_____
_____
_____
_____
_____
_____
_____
_____
_____
_____
_____
_____
_____

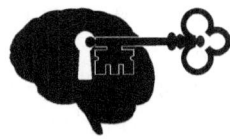

Key Two: Support

Stacie Seifrit Griffin—
Award-winning Marketing and Promotion Director, radio DJ
Authentic, creative, leader, volunteer
Hero

Bringing people together and creating communities is at the core of my passion as a volunteer supporting our public schools. When Mrs. Beachboard asked me to visit her eighth-grade class to talk about their idea for a literacy fair, I don't think either of us realized how impactful this meeting would be.

One by one, students introduced themselves. They had already divided up responsibilities; each had a long list of goals they wanted to accomplish and businesses they wanted to engage. Their ideas and voices filled the room with all of the reasons why this was so important to them. They wanted children to have access to free books in hopes they would keep reading over the summer. I had never met these students, but I knew them. I was one of them—the self-starter who was going to change the world.

Our one-hour meeting turned into weekly meetings as we created timelines, realistic ideas, effective marketing materials, job descriptions, roles, and expectations. Mrs. Beachboard's students researched and secured a location, got the proper approvals, and created a budget. These were simple, everyday tasks for me, but new ways of thinking for them. They asked a lot of questions and embraced everything.

In addition to free books, they would have games, moon bounces, food vendors, balloon sculptors, face painting, music, and more. These kids were planning a free, outdoor, community event for all ages.

With the knowledge that comes from experience, I worried for them. First-time events can have so many variables; I hoped it wouldn't rain and that another event wouldn't overshadow theirs. We pushed on. They wrote press releases, submitted letters to local businesses, and created event t-shirts, banners, and flyers. One student dedicated her entire weekend to teaching herself how to build a website. They were ready.

I should point out that all of this was happening during the busy state standardized testing time. Teachers all over the county were busy reviewing as much material as they could so students would be prepared. Mrs. Beachboard let me know that to her, this event was the perfect way to prepare her students. By encouraging critical thinking, writing, budgeting, speaking, and collaborating, she was teaching real-life experience. (I later learned that every single one of Mrs. Beachboard's students passed the test.)

The morning of the event, it was pouring down rain. Plan B ready. The students and their team of volunteers moved everything inside the school. They were well prepared.

I was out of town on business, so I arrived when the event was already in progress. I was discouraged as I drove to the school in the pouring rain. I prepared some words of wisdom about how some things are just out of your control no matter how hard you work or plan.

As I made a left into the school parking lot, my eyes teared up. The parking lot was full. The event was a huge success with families carrying books, balloons, prizes, and more as they mingled around the school.

For these students, there was no fear. They possessed a remarkable willingness to succeed. For me, the students' literacy fair was an unforgettable experience in the power of youth and the importance of a teacher empowering their dreams.

Relationships are the foundation to unlocking students. However, getting students and their families to *participate* at school is the key to unlocking a kid's broader potential. As we sat down to write about engagement, we pondered something that's been asked over and over in education: "If your students didn't have to be there, would they show up to class?" Suddenly we had an "aha!" moment—school may not be optional, but church *is*. Many kids and families in our area attend religious services. We wondered: how do churches engage their members and families? How can we get students and families engaged in the happenings of our classrooms?

Curious, I (Cathleen) decided to meet with Pastor Brad Hales. He serves as the Director of Domestic Missions for the North American Lutheran Church. A big part of his job is church renewal, which means turning around churches that struggle. Which means he knows how to turn little engagement into a lot. Interestingly enough, Pastor Brad also worked as a history teacher for many years.

It was an early afternoon when I wandered into Pastor Brad's plain but comfortable office. He greeted me with a smile. I sat on an overstuffed couch as he finished a call.

Replacing the phone in its cradle, Pastor Brad handed me a sheet of white paper. It was titled "Reflections on the Church Renewal Process" and evenly divided by bulleted lines of text. He laughed. "Once a teacher, always a teacher. I had to get my thoughts down."

I settled in and went straight to the point. "Pastor Brad, I asked for this meeting because I know you help churches that have declining memberships. Since, unlike school, church is optional, can you tell me what you use to increase engagement?"

Center On, and Don't Deviate From, a Core Message

He sat back in his chair and took a deep breath. "First, there is a reason for no growth. This list is a bunch of points that I focus on to help get people engaged. In order to get the renewal process going, I try to find out the core message that the church is focused on … In order to build growth, there has to be a foundation."

This got me thinking about how teachers have their own "why" for teaching. That's probably one of the reasons most teaching programs require their pupils to draft a teaching philosophy. Our teaching philosophies shape us at our cores. In order to have direction in the classroom, teachers need a foundation. A teaching philosophy can also give us motivation to persist during difficulties. How can we engage students and families if we don't know why we're doing it? Our "why" is the reason we lean on in tough times and sharing it can get families and students inspired to engage in our classrooms.

Sometimes, though, tough times shape our "why." I (Marynn) first wrote my philosophy of teaching while earning my master's degree in education. As instructed, I worked hard to craft a statement defining my role as a teacher. I had goals for students: content knowledge, life skills, learning styles, and combined effectiveness. It was impressive! Four years passed, and "tough times" struck. Out of the blue, I was diagnosed with sudden-onset, idiopathic kidney disease. I listened in disbelief as doctors outlined how much they didn't know about my condition. "You may wish to put your affairs in order," one gentleman suggested. "We can't say for sure whether you'll see 30 or not." I was 27.

I spent time in a hospital bed staring at a ceiling that was, no kidding, stained with blood. Later, while walking slowly through a beautiful park named for a person long dead, it struck me: no one remembers what the park's namesake was really like. So what was I doing, trying to be "perfect?" Why worry about "making" it? Even if I got famous enough to have a park named after me (doubtful), no one would know who I really was anyway! All I could possibly do was to live well *now*. I felt ashamed of the rumors I'd heard about students being afraid of me; despite feeling that I loved my kids, I knew I'd been a real bulldog—perfection or bust! No longer. That afternoon, I went home and wrote in my journal: "Live well." It became my statement of purpose in everything.

I started talking with students weekly, sometimes daily, about what it meant to live well. What kind of skills would one need to do that? What types of knowledge? How did literacy fit in? That was when passion projects in my classes took off. My kids watched me struggle through kidney treatments and side effects, and they wanted to dig in and try hard, too. Students reached out to others experiencing chronic illness and physical disability. They formed partnerships with peers they'd never met before. They taught lessons at local elementary schools. One pair of girls designed assistive gardening tools for children with physical challenges. To a man, my kids concluded that living well involved helping others. A new and improved *why* had taken root.

Build Relationships—Serve in Community

That actually leads back to my (Cathleen's) discussion with Pastor Brad. What's the next step after determining an organization's purpose? Here's a hint: it has to do with the last chapter!

"After you figure out the core message," Pastor Brad continued, "the next big idea is that relationships need to be built. The person in charge needs to serve in the community. I serve on all kinds of boards and volunteer in order to know the needs of the people and to serve in the place I'm trying to connect with."

This is a lot like teachers volunteering for clubs, sports, or other extracurriculars. By serving outside of class, we get a different view of our students. We model dedication. Kids get to see that we are there for them

> **Tip for Teacher Heroes**
>
> By all means, invest in students outside of class whenever possible! However, different seasons of your life will require varying distributions of time. Connect with your community *and* be kind to yourself, too. It can be a tough balance to strike. I would just note that teaching is not a selfish career. If you're looking to serve yourself, you're going to have a tough time building relationships with students and families.

in different capacities, and we work side by side together to accomplish something. Teachers also get to interact with a variety of families, organizations, and community leaders when they volunteer to serve. This also shows kids and families that you don't stop caring about kids when they leave the door of your classroom. This is self-sacrificial. We have to be wise about balancing care for ourselves and our families with the needs of others. Keeping that in mind, though, both Marynn and I have found major benefits of volunteering to form deeper relationships because if you care about kids outside of school it leads them to care more while they are in school.

A Positive, Optimistic Attitude

Brad's chuckling brought me back to our conversation. "Having a positive attitude while volunteering or doing anything helps build engagement too," he added. "Often we can feel like for every one foot forward, we take three steps back. Focus needs to be on growth and the positive little things. A positive attitude invites and welcomes growth."

It was nice to be reminded of this. Everyone has bad days, of course, but our actions set the tone for our relationships with students and their families. Doctor of Psychology Sherrie Bourg Carter wrote an article for *Psychology Today* in October 2012. It was titled "Emotions are Contagious—Choose Your Company Wisely." Doctor Carter pointed out that emotional contagion is a real process where we spread our emotions out into a group. If we want our classrooms to be positive places, students have to "catch" the feeling from us.

Imagine the emotional contagion on the first day of school when students enter a room full of negativity. First impressions matter, and starting with lists of rules and consequences puts everyone in a bad mood.

After all, how would we adults react if we entered a house of worship and were immediately confronted with the congregation's list of rules or book of discipline? Most of us would run away and never come back! But in our capacity as teachers, we forget what we know as people.

I know I've fallen into the first-day-of-school pattern that dictates syllabi expectations and required reading lists. In retrospect, it's amazing my students were willing to give me a second chance! Instead let's emphasize creating warm, inviting places for learning. We can teach our expectations and bring a little joy too.

Make Connections by Being Out and About

After taking a moment to think, Pastor Brad pointed to me and wagged his finger. "One of the most important steps that I tell anyone struggling to get people engaged is to visit. Make connections. I set myself a goal every week for connecting to members, families, and people of the community. A big part of engaging families and students is reaching out to them. Meet people where they are and remember if you go see them, they'll come see you."

As he said this, my mind reeled. A lot of the things on his to-do list I've made an effort towards, but I've never set visitation goals with students' families. It's intimidating. But here's my way of thinking: when we teach children, we become part of their families' lives for a time. If we are to truly know students, we need to know the support networks they live within.

In the first few months of each new school year, I do a project where I invite families to come see their children present. It's an opportunity to connect with 100+ families. We shouldn't stop inviting in parent volunteers once a child passes elementary school. They say it takes a village to raise a child, so if you want to be effective you have to know who is in their village. Of course, time is an issue when planning any kind of visit, but here's good news: visits don't have to be physical!

One of the ways I like to end every school day is by making three positive phone calls to parents during my drive home. I pre-load each family's phone number into my cell before getting on the road, and I give updates on children's progress along with positive comments. This is a small way to get myself in the door of kids' lives. In a month, I might make 60 new connections with families. Those families can also discuss concerns and problems with me. We avoid conflict and communicate more clearly. We become allies. Yes, families sometimes approach me with more needs than they would have otherwise, but doors swing both ways. Often, those same folks help contribute towards the needs of my classroom. Like Pastor Brad said, if I call them, they'll call me.

> **Tip for Teacher Heroes**
>
> It can be tough to pick up a new habit, even one you know is good for you and your students! Here's a helpful hack Cathleen learned from her personal trainer while she was working on losing weight: you can gain new habits by embedding them with old ones. Want to make positive phone calls but just can't seem to fit them in with everything else? Add "make calls" to another afternoon or evening routine you're already doing like walking the dog, exercising, cleaning, or cooking. And when you do chat with parents, ask if they'd mind you keeping their phone number for the year; it really comes in handy if you need to reach them quickly on another occasion!

"In an age of advancing technology, a lot of people feel underconnected," Pastor Brad continued as he leaned back in his chair. "It's more important than ever to have phone and face-to-face meetings. Families long to feel needed and connected." I couldn't agree more. Tell me if this pattern sounds familiar: a PTA is robust in elementary school, waning in middle school, and all but gone in high school. Why? Many parents I've spoken with say they feel like they're no longer needed in the upper grades. Some of that expectation for students' independence is age-appropriate, but a lot of it goes back to school culture. "Families long to feel needed *and* connected." What kind of connections might we create with something more memorable than email or automated text messages? Let's show families how much we value them by sharing the only precious thing we all have: time.

Confront Conflict "Head On"

Pastor Brad leaned forward with his hands folded and looked back to the notes he made. "One of the big problems with churches that are struggling is that they have trouble brewing. With big problems, no growth can occur. One of the things I've learned is that conflict should be tackled head on and as soon as possible. Conflicts deserve face-to-face meetings where a solution can be worked out. 'People problems' hurt growth."

He makes a great point. The more people we engage, the more likely we are to run into differences. Disagreements can stem from families, students, staff members, or community members. Although this can be upsetting, try to remember that conflict is a normal part of life. After all, siblings argue despite having a lot in common; how much more likely that near strangers will find things to disagree about? We find it helpful to look at "conflict" as "an opportunity to problem solve." Much like Pastor Brad said, timeliness and medium are key to creating a positive, engaging environment for solutions. So is our mindset going in.

> **Tip for Teacher Heroes**
>
> Those of us who've experienced painful conflicts in the past might, understandably, be hesitant to try this "immediate, head-on" approach. Here's something to help bolster your confidence: think about what you've learned from past experiences, and then plan your exit strategy.
>
> The first part is important because *you survived* whatever it was that hurt. It may have been a close call, but you're here today. How did that happen? What can you do to survive even better next time? Then, consider what you'll do if a situation gets out of hand in the future. Where will you go? How will you get there? Who can you call for help?

Sometimes, of course, it is good to walk away from problems for a bit. Rash emotions ebb and fade with time. However, avoiding conflict for too long comes with its own dangers. My (Cathleen's) grandma used say, "Problems are like a shaken-up soda can. Open them too soon and they may explode, but wait too long and the solutions go flat." There is a sweet spot with problem solving. We've got to balance taking time to breathe with gathering our nerves and jumping in.

Here's bad news for the passive aggressive among us: email usually isn't going to end a conflict. The trouble is that it puts a screen between me and the problem. I can't actively listen with all of my senses if my discussion partner is behind a wall. Even though I sometimes feel safer hunkering behind my keyboard, it's inefficient. No more than 50% of conflicts I've addressed through email have reached resolution that way; we nearly always end up needing to schedule an in-person meeting. On the other hand, conflicts I've addressed via live conferences have successfully resolved about 95% of the time. By swallowing both my pride and my fear, I open myself up to a more positive interaction overall when I invite folks to simply talk things out. Phone calls are a close second in terms of efficiency, but they still lack the power of facial expression and body language.

Pastor Brad concluded by pointing back to his paper, "By dealing with problems face to face, you show that you value the person enough to listen, empathize, and respond."

Build on Your Strengths

A bit worn out by the depth and breadth of our discussion, Pastor Brad and I took a moment to grab some coffee. Refreshed, I asked, "Once you've laid the groundwork, so to speak, how do you go about the business of actually *building* engaged members? Or a classroom community?"

Pastor Brad laughed. "It's easy to hone in on problems and the negative. To grow, there has to be a shift in focus. Sounds easy, right? It's one of those things that is and isn't at the same time. You can attract a crowd not by emphasizing what you don't have, but what you do. For example, when I came to the church here in Virginia, people told me to focus on growing our youth program. At the time, we had a large senior population and few teens. Instead of focusing on what we didn't have at the time, I decided to focus on the senior population. We created adult bible schools and a place for seniors to meet and socialize. The church grew larger and thrived because we were emphasizing our assets—our current population!"

Every year, we teachers get new groups of kids and families to interact with. This is the biggest reason that classrooms have to change from year to year—the "assets" alter! Often we focus on deficits instead of strengths. If we are to foster a positive school environment, this has to change. We can build relationships while taking stock of the assets available to us. Everyone has a gift.

As teachers, we have a large community of skills and support at our fingertips. It's our job to look at what we have and bring it together to benefit our classrooms; it might mean lessons in marketing (see Stacie's story at the beginning of this chapter) or free t-shirts for an event (printed by a mom who was passionate about design). Anything is possible when we see the world of potential in each new person we meet.

Remember: It's Always About the People

Pastor Brad leveled his gaze and stunned me with one of his last thoughts. "I may not remember all the things I have done over the years," he said quietly, "but I always remember the people I meet. At the end of the day, my job is always about the people."

It's in this that I see how similar our professions truly are. At the end of the day, a teacher's job is to help people. We have the ability to open doors and hearts. We can renew the meaning of lifelong learning. We can lead by example and model reaching out. Engagement is contagious: if we show caring outside of the classroom we will get intrinsic caring and engagement inside the classroom. How might all of our classrooms change for the better this year if we embrace the power of working together?

Unlocking "Support:" Big Ideas

Locks:	Keys:
Engagement is difficult.	Center on a core message and celebrate small wins.
Teaching is isolating.	Serve in the community and create connections for you and your students.
Families don't engage.	Make connections and be "out and about."
Problems are everywhere.	Confront conflict "head on" because the faster the problem ends, the quicker you return to peace.
There are not enough resources.	Build on your strengths and use what you have to create a domino effect.
There's too many things to do.	Remember, at the end of the day it's always about the people.

So what? Unlock student potential by showing there is heroic strength in unity.

Reflection on Engaging People

This is space for you to reflect and write your own thoughts on community engagement. Have a great idea or insight? Please share at www.unlockingheroes.com

Key Three: Strength

Niamh Kierans—Student
Driven, feminist, frank, impartial
Hero

For about a week I had been preparing a speech to make to the Fauquier Board of Supervisors at a public budget hearing. A month before, if you had asked me why I was doing this, I would have had no idea. That's something that happened a lot in my eighth-grade English class, becoming very passionate about something that you just learned about a few minutes ago.

Our county's school system hadn't been granted the budget it requested for a very long time, and it was showing. Parts of the schools were falling apart, and not many interesting field trips or activities could happen because of lack of funding. Our teachers were trying very hard to make it work, but there came a point where there needed to be change.

My English teacher, Mrs. Beachboard, had recently introduced the budget problem to our fourth-period class. Of course, being the teacher that she is, she invited one of the members of our county's Board of Supervisors to come and let our class bombard him with questions. After his visit, though he did answer a lot of our questions, we were not satisfied with what we had learned. So, obviously, the next thing to do was to have the entire class attend and give speeches at the public budget hearing.

One of the major things we had learned in class that year was the "Trifecta of Awesome," being *logos* (logic), *pathos* (emotional appeal), and *ethos* (ethical appeal). Our teacher encouraged each of us to use our speech to target one of those three points. However, she specifically asked me to target logic because she felt that that type of persuasion was one of my strengths and she wanted to see me use it in a real-world situation.

When I arrived at the high school (where the hearing was being held), I was nervous and unsure of myself. There were many people in the audience as our teachers had spread the word that everyone should come and voice their opinions. My hands were shaky and I felt uneasy. But when Mrs. Beachboard came up to me before the hearing and told me how excited she was to hear me speak, I knew that this really was important and that this speech could make a difference.

So, when I was called, I made what I would consider one of my best speeches ever. I felt sure of myself, knowing that my teacher was supporting me whole-heartedly. Many of the other students from my school and parents from my county spoke that night, all of us speaking out against what we saw as wrong.

In the end, our school was able to receive a much higher budget for the next year and years after, meaning better technology and safety measurements, and overall experiences for all of the students of Fauquier county would improve. Even though it was a team effort, I still felt like a hero that day. Not only for making a change in my community, but for making a change in myself.

When my (Cathleen's) father was a small boy, he contracted the polio virus. It destroyed the muscles in his legs. Doctors told my grandmother my father would never walk and would be sick all of his life. Little did the doctors know, my father feared being a burden on his large family; he was determined to be healthy. He worked on strengthening his legs daily, walking with braces and crutches. My father wanted nothing more than to walk and be like other kids.

Sadly, the polio had severely damaged his left leg. No matter how hard he tried, his left leg remained weak. However, his right leg started gaining muscle. Daily he pushed his good leg harder and harder. My grandmother used to tell me that he would walk steps constantly until he was ready to collapse with exhaustion. Within a few years, he was walking. His left leg never got bigger. My father ended up with one massive, herculean leg and one leg that looked like a bean pole. In the end, the strength of his right leg allowed him to walk and do what doctors thought was impossible. My dad fell occasionally because his weak leg gave out, but he never let it stop him. He wore volleyball knee pads to avoid injury—the falls were worth the independence of walking. Falling was a part of his life that he knew would happen. When it did, he quietly picked himself up, relying on his stronger leg to keep going.

My father used one source of strength to compensate for an equal but opposite weakness. His story reminds me that in education, we sometimes forget to leave space for weakness. No one is good at everything. Marynn and I both believe, though, that every person is good at something. Identifying strengths won't fix kids' problems. It might be enough, though, to help them keep walking in difficult times.

Confidence and Courage

Think about your favorite teacher. Picture him or her in your mind. What made this teacher great? His activities? Her classroom environment? Or was it the fact that this teacher helped develop your strengths, confidence, and courage in yourself? There is power in helping people find their own value. The duty of teachers is not to change students, but to bring out the strengths inside them. That's why in empowered classrooms, kids come first and content comes second.

> **Tip for Teacher Heroes**
>
> Regarding content: teach it. Obviously! We're not advocating that teachers abandon ship (or whatever metaphor you care to use). All we're trying to say is that teachers teach students, who are in-process people. Our content is the tool we use to help shape those people. It's a matter of both and, not either or.

One of the most precious items in my classroom is a digital folder on my computer titled "Strength." Inside, there's a subfolder for each student I'm currently teaching. I keep a record of students' strengths as I find them in letters from home, classroom observations, and conversations with school staff. In a world of participation trophies, I strive to show students that their unique abilities set them apart. My dream is that every school system in America would take on the challenge of knowing students' strengths *and* weaknesses. You know how we keep records for kids' discipline incidents and interactions with admin? Let's add one more page to school records. We could call it something like "Profile of Student's Strengths," and everyone in the educational team could add to it over the years. Imagine the impact if graduates received not only a diploma but a personalized list of personal strengths upon graduation. What if that list originated in kindergarten? What a way to track progress! What a tool to encourage the pursuit of passions!

My (Cathleen's) middle school students want desperately to blend in. Ironically, the variety of problems in our world demands they leverage their unique abilities. By keeping track of individual strengths, I have a jumping-off point to empower my kiddos. I categorize strengths so I can record everything, from Joey's amazing basketball skills to Gabby's masterful public-speaking abilities. I know that keeping track of 96+ students is a lot, but at the end of the day, I'm preparing my kids to find a passion and purpose for their lives. Showing someone what they're good at is motivational. Our favorite teachers taught us this long before we recognized our need to know it.

On the other hand, without the will to act, ability is nothing. If our students are going to live boldly, they need a chance to be brave. My dad would not have gained the courage to walk by taking a test on muscles and how to strengthen them; he needed purpose and persistence. Dad knew he was going to fall when he tried to walk. The risk was worthwhile because of his purpose. Remember when you learned to ride a bike? Falling was an option. No one could take the risk for you, but no one else was going to receive the joy of riding, either. "Just like riding a bike" is powerful because it's one of the first times that most of us experience this truth: learning involves solitary failure, reflection, and the willingness *to get back up and try again*. Students need the same things my father did: a purpose for learning and the persistence to push through failure. Guess where they learn that? Experience.

Academic content can work the same way. Take plumbing, for example. One Sunday morning, years ago, my sink began growling *loudly*. I made it downstairs just in time to witness the pipes let go. Water was everywhere. The idea of getting a plumber on an emergency call seemed ludicrous and expensive; my budget was tight, and I couldn't afford it. I knew exactly nothing about kitchen plumbing, much less the tools involved, but I had purpose and an excellent reason for persistence. I might fail at fixing the sink, but it was worth the risk to avoid bankruptcy by learning plumbing. After watching hours of YouTube videos, I eventually figured out the problem. (And gained a whole new respect for plumbers.) I also discovered that I'm fairly handy with a monkey wrench. I would never have gained confidence in my skill at plumbing if it hadn't been for this trial by fire. Students need something similar: the chance to learn, explore, and fail forward with new skills on their own.

For my (Marynn's) students, that's where passion projects come in. Passion projects, also called Genius Hour and 20% Time, are essentially teacher-assigned opportunities for students to explore and pursue something they're passionate about for a specified amount of time. Then

> **Tip for Teacher Heroes**
>
> Start small, friend, and remember, "Small changes add up to big results." One inspirational poster reads, "A journey of a thousand miles begins with a single step." Cathleen and I have big stories to tell because we've spent years building up our repertoire of strength builders. I (Marynn) am only just beginning to teach in a fully project-based learning (PBL)-based classroom because I decided five years ago that it would best help me help students, and I've been moving in that direction ever since. I'm not at all sure that there is one "right way" in teaching, but I am sure that when you begin seeking the *best* in your kids, you're going to be amazed.

students share their learning with an authentic audience. In the past three years, I've had freshmen write novellas, run marathons, learn new languages, and experiment (to varying degrees of success) with a wide variety of handicrafts and culinary arts. There are hundreds of stories I could tell, but it's best to start small. Let me tell you about Kacie's illustrations.

Kacie was a silent watcher when I met her. She had the flair of a natural artist, but when she tried to speak, it was as though a sponge absorbed her words. For a few months, she entirely avoided looking me in the eye. Mumbling and writing were her two main forms of communication. Occasionally, though, something would get Kacie fired up. When that happened, she'd speak out confidently, forgetting or ignoring her usual petrified silence in front of her peers until their attention brought her back to herself, at which point she'd clam up again. The moments were few and far between, but they made me believe in the power of Kacie's passion.

Our passion project theme that semester was "help somebody." The parameters were few and broad. Students were to find a way to connect what they cared about with the mission of tangibly improving somebody's life in a way they could then describe in a TED talk-style presentation at the end of the year. I was certain that this would be a massive challenge for Kacie, since all she really seemed to care about was drawing pictures. I couldn't imagine a way that drawing could help someone, other than the artist him- or herself. How wrong I was!

On project pitch day, students came to class more or less prepared to pitch their project ideas to their classmates. In a 30–45-second spiel, each individual or pair explained the gist of what they hoped to achieve in the following 10 weeks. We sat our desks in a big "long table" formation at the middle of the room and began. Soon it was Kacie's turn. With a visible gulp, Kacie half-whispered her decision to use her art to help students with mental health disorders. "I'm going to interview people about their depression and stuff and then draw what they describe to help them see for themselves what it's like to live that way and maybe to help them see a way out. I want to do this because I'm sick, too, and I wish someone would do this for me, and …" Kacie's voice died away. Her eyes widened and her breath came in gasps. As it happens, I have a few mental health issues of my own, so I recognized the signs immediately: Kacie was slipping into a panic attack.

I panicked a little, too. If Kacie was embarrassed about having an attack in front of her frightened classmates, how would she recover? Could I bring her back down to reality without causing a scene? And how, oh how, was she ever going to be able to complete her project, much less share her results in a public speech? I didn't know what to do. But thanks to years and years of battling my own depressive and anxious symptoms, I *felt* it.

"Kacie." I leaned across the table. "Look at me." She did. Her eyes were huge, and her hands were trembling. "Your brain is trying to run away with you, Kace," I said calmly. "Remember how we've talked before about the thinking, feeling, and surviving brain? Your surviving brain is kicking in. I need you to tell it to knock it off, please. It's got to listen to you, because it's your brain, and you're in charge. Breathe out. You're ok." Miraculously, the moment passed. Kacie released a huge sigh and seemed to come back to herself. The presentation pitches continued. Crisis averted.

Later that week, I met with Kacie during study hall to talk about her project. We didn't discuss her panicked moment in class, but we did discuss how to conduct interviews sensitively, who she was going to talk to, and how to know when to get help from an adult. Kacie shared a little about her mental health challenges. She spoke again about her conviction that seeing symptoms put down on paper could help teens understand what they were dealing with and how to talk about it. With some hesitation, and a lot of support from the school nurse, counseling department, and Kacie's family, we decided to move forward with her project.

A few months later, it was presentation day. Kacie arrived to class dressed in a stunning blue silk dress overlaid with black lace and carrying four canvases draped in cloth. She shook visibly in her chair while waiting for her turn to speak. When it came, though, she stood strong and still. As the feedback forms revealed later, very few people saw Kacie's hands tremble while she spoke; they were transfixed instead by her portraits of students surrounded by the effects of depression, anxiety, eating disorders, and self-harm. In clear and simple terms, Kacie taught her audience about the impact of mental health on students' daily lives and the difference between various disorders. She also taught ways to seek help.

Kacie ended her presentation to a standing ovation. She never faltered. By speaking out for others' weakness, Kacie had found a way to tap into her own strength. The next semester, she tried out for the school's color guard team. Then she joined the technical crew for drama club and put her artistic skills to further good use. Last I heard, she was planning to attend college to pursue a degree in clinical counseling. Weakness combined with courage can transform into strength.

Encouragement

The question is, will we have the courage to choose transformation? Every day, everyone has a choice: maintain or grow. As humans, we prefer to maintain homeostasis. All of us are genetically programmed towards stasis. It's in our DNA. We're comfortable when we stay the same. To add to the difficulty of choosing change, building strength is slow. We have to fight to do things differently. When we say as teachers that we've got to encourage students to embrace their strengths, we mean the literal meaning of the French word *"encourage"*—from Old French *encoragier*, "make strong, hearten," from *en-* "make, put in" + *corage* "courage, heart" (definition from www.etymonline.com/word/encourage) We, as teachers, need to help students be strong to push back from accepting a life that's ordinary and to fight for extraordinary.

Dear reader, when we encourage students to discover or embrace their strengths, we do so with the knowledge that building strength is a long, slow process of gradual change. Do you think that when my (Cathleen's) father began climbing stairs in his house, he suddenly saw the muscles in his leg grow? Of course not! I couldn't tell you how many thousands of stairs my dad climbed to finally walk unassisted. On the third day of my weight loss journey, I didn't look a bit different than I did the day before I started. Kacie didn't overcome her fear of speaking in public in a day or even a week. I only learned to fix my sink by spending hours watching instructional videos. Only by embracing weakness as an opportunity and not a limit can we begin to discover strength. After all, weakness in people is a ripe soil for strength to slowly grow.

Hear this now: Change. Takes. Time. Helping students discover their own strengths will, too. That's ok. That's how it's supposed to work. The important thing is to begin and then refuse to quit. That's how you strengthen a polio-affected leg, fix a broken pipe, encourage a fearful speaker, and lose a hundred pounds. As teachers dedicated to unlocking the heroes in our students, it's our daily mission to train the next generation to use their strengths to get better daily Please, let us encourage you (because yeah, this is going to be hard, and it's going to take a long time!) to seek out the strengths in your students. Then, give those precious boys and girls every opportunity you possibly can so they can begin their journeys towards personal heroism.

Our duty as teachers is to improve the lives of our students, and what better way to do that then show kids that the strength and power to become great lie within them?

Unlocking Strength: Big Ideas

Locks:	Keys:
Everyone will face a weakness or difficult task.	Allow students to find courage and don't be too quick to save the day. Students need a chance to authentically struggle to discover their own abilities.
Teachers expect every student to become a master of all content and subject matter.	Students need to be encouraged to problem solve using their strengths when facing difficult concepts or content.

So what? In a world where new problems are created daily, students will need courage, strength, and passion to face the unknown.

Quick Resources for Strength
1. **Portfolio of Strength**
    One of the most valuable things I do for students is keep a portfolio of strengths for each student. It contains observations, parent feedback, and student reflections from the year. In a spreadsheet I list evidence of strengths from the work the students do during the year and I add to it. To start the portfolio I use the "In a Million Words or Less" in Chapter 1 to gain feedback from parents on given strengths and talents. When school starts I ask students to reflect and make a list of what they think they are "good at." I add these to the list of strengths for the student.
    I take this list and divide it up into categories for each student: Social, Athleticism, Artistic Merits, Hobbies/Talents, Mechanical,

and Other. One student may have a list with evidence of the following strengths: artistic, with drawing realistic pictures, strong public speaker, great at puzzles, large knowledge base of the outdoors, great mediator in groups (and with their siblings at home); athletic talent with basketball. I divide the strengths into categories and constantly update the list. Strength portfolios allow teachers and students to quickly utilize strengths to compensate for weakness. Giving a student a list of strengths gives them something to be proud of and allows them to have something to build off to develop new strengths. Imagine a world where each grade level passes on a portfolio of strengths that not only helps build rapport with kids, but gives teachers a jumping-off point.

2. **Passion Projects**

    Lots of folks have done invaluable work helping teachers make passion projects a reality in their classrooms. If you're interested in firing up student motivation and engagement by implementing independent, inquiry-based learning, we recommend starting with materials created by the following: Laura Randazzo (she was Marynn's internet PBL mentor), A.J. Jiuliani (Marynn used his materials verbatim for a while), and Trevor McEnzy (whose book Cathleen adored).

3. **Problem Speed Dating**

    Sometimes we learn our strength by facing new problems and this allows students to see the value in relying on others, building classroom bonding. Once a week students can bring a problem from the world or their own life to class. Students turn in their problems the night before to the teacher. The next day, after the problems have been looked at by the teacher, they are given out randomly to the class. The job of each student is to be a solution collector.

Reflection on Strength

A page for you to reflect and write your own thoughts on strength. Have a great idea or insight? Feel free to share at www.unlockingheroes.com

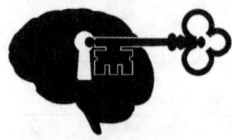

Key Four: Willpower

Connor Bellemare—Student
Creative, witty, reserved, unpresuming
Hero

I'm Connor Bellemare, and I did three different passion projects last semester: string figures, basic sewing, and making a metallurgy forge. Why didn't I do a big project the first two times? Well, I just didn't know what to do. It was supposed to start small and grow bigger. That's how I saw it, and I wasn't sure how to set a small goal that would lead into a bigger one. I'm not very extracurricular. I pretty much only do school and that's it, so I've never really done small things that built up to big ones. This whole experience was very new for me, very different.

My first passion project was just a novelty, something I could use as a fun party trick. With the second, I didn't learn too much, either. I could maybe stitch a button back on. I didn't do very well with either one. Not only did I not hit my goals, but my speeches were unplanned. I wasn't prepared. That's because I've always been bad at getting out of bed and doing anything at all. This was no different; I've always had some kind of laziness and apathy. So I was kind of torn—I felt bad about the fact that I wasn't achieving at my highest level, but I also didn't want to be working in the first place.

The forge project, on the other hand, felt a lot bigger. It was like, "I've been wanting to do this for years." I saw a video and it looked awesome. I'd always wanted to build one, so actually having a goal that was big and amazing and something that I really wanted for myself … that got me over the hump of tending to be a little lazy.

Once I got working, there was one point where I thought, "Oh man, that's going to be expensive. I'm screwed. The project is dead." I was really despairing a little bit. It happened when my first crucible broke. I made a mistake putting a circle of coals around it. One of them fell in by accident. It was too hot. The crucible wasn't meant to be at that temperature, so it busted open. It bent, and then it just fell out of the forge. By itself, that wasn't such a big deal. I'd already ordered another one, which was better. I wasn't so upset about the crucible itself, but I was worried for the forge. If molten metal got in there, it might have been ruined. I also didn't know if some of the aluminum was melted at the bottom of the crucible. If it was and I pulled it out, some might spill. There's air pockets on the ground and on the pavement. Spilled aluminum would heat it up at such high temperatures, it would expand and send hot metal everywhere. That was my biggest worry. Most of the time, though, it wasn't that dangerous. My dad worked with me five days a week. (He wasn't there when the crucible broke.) He was my cheerleader and helped keep me on track.

Over time, I learned that I needed to not procrastinate nearly so much. That's what I'd tell someone trying to reach a big goal or do a big project: you need to stay consistent, both with when you work and how you're doing it. Consistency kept me focused on the task. It helped me see where I was and where I needed to get to. For example, to keep myself on track for the forge project, I made sure I worked on it at least 30 minutes a day at the same time every day. Keeping a consistent schedule helped me take on a big challenge and push myself beyond what I thought I could do. Has it impacted my life afterward? Yes, 100%. I feel like I can do anything now.

With the support of my students, I (Cathleen) lost 100 pounds and found a new way to live. There's an element to that victory which I left unconsidered for many years: willpower. I lacked self-control in my diet and had very weak willpower to change at the start of my weight loss journey. With seven children, it was easier to snack on junk while multitasking instead of dutifully watching what I ate. My environment made it hard to make any lasting changes to my bad habits. There were snacks in my car, drive-thru happy meals for my family, and a comforting stash of chocolate in my desk at school. I wanted to lose weight, but I lacked the self-control to do it. What changed? I gained a stronger willpower. How? Through visualizing success, scaffolding goals, improving my mood, forming new habits, and planning for days of failure.

But what's the point? This is a book about student empowerment, after all. Why dedicate an entire chapter to willpower? The point of this chapter is to help you equip students to engage by taking ownership of their learning. After all, educators can't impact students' "nature or nurture." We have no influence over their homes. But teachers *can* train students to strengthen power of will. It's a great leveler.

Willpower is one important element of educational equity. Teachers can't change children's genetics or environment but can guide children to strengthen self-control. At least two major psychological studies have demonstrated that childhood self-control predicts future successes. ("A gradient of childhood self-control predicts health, wealth, and public safety." Moffitt et al.: www.pnas.org/content/108/7/2693). Therefore, educators' efforts to improve students' self-control may have the greatest impact on students' future victories. After all, what is traditional schooling really for if not a strengthening of children's will? Why is it that holding a high school diploma or equivalent is critical to gaining employment in this country? Willpower. When my adopted son chose to briefly drop out of school, he was shocked and appalled that he couldn't get a job. No diploma? No certificate of adequate willpower. Most admirable achievements in American society include an element of truly impressive drive. Professional athletes and performers spend countless hours practicing. Doctors and lawyers persist through years and years of schooling. Authors and artists spend hours buried in tedium that most folks simply don't want to withstand. It all comes back to willpower.

So when we tell you that helping your students develop their "willpower muscles" is one of the best things you can do for them, it's not for nothing. No matter your context, willpower matters for your kids. It gives them power when they feel powerless. It is their best tool for making good choices—and acting on them. Willpower will power students' ability to engage. That's the point.

Visualization and Belief

The students who wanted to help me get healthy began by giving me the gift of belief. One of the greatest tools they used was visualization. Immediately after I swore to lose weight, several students found ModelMyDiet.com, a website that simulated physical changes which would take place as I began to eat well and exercise. Students helped me input my current weight and modified the example avatar so it looked like me. Then we typed in my goal weight. For the first time, I was able to visualize what losing 10, 15, and 20 pounds would do to my body. As the old saying goes, seeing is believing. When I saw it, I started to believe I could actually look like the woman in the pictures. We printed them out, one for each drop of five pounds, and hung them behind my desk. My willpower increased drastically because I could visualize what success would look like for me; suddenly, it felt like my goals were within reach.

Thinking back on it, I realize all actions begin in the imagination. When I grab a cup of water, I imagine doing the action before actually reaching out my hand. Being able to visualize achieving goals is important. If a person cannot imagine herself in a situation, she won't do anything to prepare for it. The second part of the process, believing what you've visualized, is equally important. Because I believe the image in my mind, I act and attain my goal of picking up the cup of water. The process happens again, instantaneously, when I decide to take a drink from the cup. If I thought I couldn't grasp the glass, raise it, and drink, I probably wouldn't try. Like most other parts of our bodies, willpower gets stronger the more we use it. And *that* requires visualizing success and believing it enough to try.

Visualization and the belief that follows are powerful because they set our expectations. We use them every day for every action. They have the potential to help us reach our goals, like when my (Cathleen's) students helped me visualize the stages of losing weight. Misapplied, they can also hold us back. Marynn and I think this happens far too often in most classrooms. Students' visions of themselves, which are often based on negative prior experiences, can constrict their willpower. Remember: if a student can't see himself doing something, he's almost certainly not going to try to accomplish it.

Scaffolding Goals for a Purpose

In order for students to practice using their will, we need to give them time to imagine what they want to do with it—time to visualize. This may mean helping kids "remove their blindfolds." We can help students imagine impossibilities becoming real. Then, when they have in mind a picture of what success might look like, we've got to help them believe it. That means having goals. Goals require an action plan. I help my kids strengthen their willpower in lots of ways, but one of my favorites is called "Who."

The activity is simple. Students close their eyes and think of people they admire. They then isolate the positive qualities those people possess and use those characteristics to create a picture of themselves 30 years in the future as the person they want to be. Students then record a list of characteristics that make up the future version of themselves. Then, students record the characteristics of their future self and choose one to focus on.

Goals help increase willpower because they make progress measurable. After all, if you come to a street that has a detour, you don't just stop your trip. You know where you're headed, and much like a GPS that is angry at your wrong turn, you will start recalculating your route. Perhaps you've heard the popular weight loss advice to "set small goals and celebrate success." It's becoming common wisdom because goals help you see how far you've already come. We can help our students see that even though things may stop them, they can always recalculate to reach their visualized destination.

Having students set goals for content with their future self in mind should be a priority in classrooms. Often kids ask how content relates to their lives. When the situation is reversed and kids are asked, "How does learning _____ move you closer to who you want to become?" their answers attach personal meaning to the unit of study. With the right question, teachers can help students take ownership of creating meaning for content. Notice, though, that the question doesn't say "to the job you want." We need to move away from asking about how content relates to students' careers. This is something my son Xander discovered.

> **Tip for Teacher Heroes**
>
> It's true that success breeds success. Boost students' confidence by guiding them to set measurable, easily achievable goals at the beginning of this process. Otherwise, you risk discouragement and demoralization, which is an entirely different kettle of fish!

Xander loves to read. He's interested in many careers, especially becoming a librarian. Earlier this fall, he was excelling in English class, but in Math he brought home almost failing test grades. The crazy thing was that he understood the concepts. His problem was that he rushed through tests so he could finish and return to reading. When I asked him to explain his low scores, Xander responded, "Mom, I'm not going to need the Pythagorean theorem to become a librarian." It struck me that many, maybe most, students believe this, too: that school's purpose is to prepare children for employment. Therefore, in their minds, all learning goals and classes should be centralized on future careers.

After thinking for a moment, I asked Xander, "If that's the case, why did you bother to learn magic for your passion project last month? It doesn't deal with being a librarian, either." He saw the parallel I was drawing.

With a smirk, Xander said, "I learned magic because I thought it would be cool."

"So, why learn things just for a job?" I smiled.

It took a few minutes for Xander to puzzle through that one. "I guess," he said slowly, "we learn things to connect with others. Like to make them happy. And to understand them, too. I didn't realize how hard magic was until I started trying to learn it. Now I feel like I have a connection with magicians. I know how hard they work, so I understand them a little bit."

Much like my son Xander, students need to see that knowledge is a tool to connect people. We may not be good at all subjects, but we can attempt to learn with the intent of becoming more well informed. By doing this, we are showing that the purpose of learning is to create a bridge between one person and another. Setting goals based on who they want to be helps students see that school is a tool to help them become a better version of themselves. Kids need to see that all content is equally important, and learning doesn't stop with employment.

If Xander were to just set goals around his career, he wouldn't see the value of learning the Pythagorean theorem. After our talk, he set a goal to try harder to understand Math because it will help him connect to other people (especially the new friend who's volunteered to be his tutor). It takes a lot of self-control for Xander to slow down and concentrate in Math class. Sometimes he meets his goal, and sometimes he struggles, but he knows he's becoming a better version of himself. Xander now has a personalized purpose for learning the content, and by setting goals, he feels more in control. He is realizing that he is in charge of his education. That's why taking the time to create goals is important. As students meet each one, their willpower is strengthened and their "who" is manifested. When was the last time you reached a small goal you'd set for yourself? Do you remember the pride and sense of accomplishment that carried you through the rest of your day? That's what we're trying to create for our learners. With each skill gained, kids witness their future self materializing before their very eyes. Soon the "who" they want to become is within their grasp.

The Power of Positivity

In a study summarized by Dr. Cummins on PsychologyToday.com, researchers discovered that "inducing good mood" via things like surprise gifts and comedy videos powerfully counteracted the effects of depleted willpower. When study participants were cheered and encouraged, they resisted tempting sweets better than subjects who weren't cheered up. The phenomenon is true in teachers' lives, too. At least, "good mood induction" is what my parent–teacher organization aims for when they deliver thank you notes on days I'm scheduled to proctor standardized tests! I've also had the good fortune to work with colleagues who've instituted "secret pals." There's nothing like seeing a gift waiting at my classroom door to refill my willpower in the morning.

Though it's not often financially feasible, small acts of kindness like that can really encourage students, too. Some years ago, I attended a summer professional development conference that ran for several days. I was shocked by how exhausted I was by the end of each day. It made me grumpy and unwilling to engage in even excellent interactive presentations. "No wonder my students are such zombies by last period," I thought. "I am, too!" It was an epiphany. If I struggled to maintain my mood and will to learn after seven hours, how could I expect more from high school students?

I now keep a small collection of dollar store "giftables" in my supply closet. Once in a while, I'll pull one out and offer a gift to celebrate a significant life event. Activities focused on gratitude, thankfulness, and humor can serve a similar purpose, and they're free! Games are good, too. Many students enjoy "the high five game" (we race around the room trying to collect the most high fives in 10 seconds) and things like "wink murder" or "heads-up seven-up" as brain breaks. Sacrificing a few minutes for positivity nearly always pays huge dividends. Like the researchers found, students and teachers are better able to leverage willpower when they're feeling cheerful.

A Process for Building Helpful Habits

We use willpower daily. Different amounts are "spent" or used up depending on the difficulty of each task. Habits are helpful because they allow our brains to take a break. Think about driving a car, for instance. When most people first learn to drive, they have to think about getting in the car, starting it, how to safely reverse, and all the rest. After a few years of experience, that same process becomes much easier. Similarly, forming positive habits allows our brains to follow familiar patterns. This conserves precious willpower. The human brain prefers to "work smarter, not harder," so we use habits as much as possible. Students need to be made aware that their habits will either set them up for a smooth drive or make their journey intolerable.

There are a lot of habits, or familiar patterns, we could teach students. However, these three are critical for building willpower: finding your baseline, noticing trends, and hooking new habits on to old ones. These three things give us the means to take control of what we do daily. When we teach kids how to notice and change their actions, we give them the means to improve the way they live.

It's important not to start everything at once, though. When I (Cathleen) started out to lose weight with my student coaches, they read articles on how to help me. One explained most people give up on losing weight because they attempt to change too many habits at once. Weight loss patients do better when they focus on one thing at a time. It's the same reason why texting and driving is frequently prohibited; when drivers scatter their focus, they end up wrecked on the side of the road. That's why we've got to implement one new habit at a time. Take on too many, and you're practically guaranteed to fail.

With that said, the most helpful "habit-forming habit" to learn (and teach) first is finding a baseline. To lose weight, I learned to focus on what I was eating before changing anything. I practiced honing my focus by logging my food at every meal and snack time. After about a week, it had become automatic. (I still track my food daily just out of habit.) The same process works for students. Let's say you're working with a child who has set a goal to read more but "hates reading." Before changing anything, you've got to help that child find his baseline. Perhaps you'll help him set up a "reading diary" the way I had a "food diary." Your student could track every time he has to read anything, anywhere, any time, for a few days. (I've also had students keep track of how many times they called out in class, etc.) Once that becomes easy enough to be habitual, you can add on other elements: *how did you feel about that reading? How long did it take? What was it for?* And so on. With that data in hand, your student now has what he needs to see his baseline performance. The more you help students practice setting their baseline, the more automatic it will become.

Tip for Teacher Heroes

Please note: teaching students these three foundational habits *requires* that they have goals they want to achieve. It's a process of teaching kids skills to build their ownership and independence, not a classroom management technique. This will *never work* if *you* set goals for your students. They've got to own the mission—you're just helping them accomplish it.

The second habit-forming habit is this: noticing trends. When I logged what I ate, I saw patterns and was able to recognize the things that were holding me back from reaching my health goals. Students can do this, too, but most will probably need support from you at the beginning of the process. Be ready to look over students' baselines with them to help them notice patterns. Have a few good questions at the ready. "What jumps out at you? What fits your expectations? Why do you think _____?" Guiding students through this process of analysis and reflection is an art form. It's going to take practice, and each conversation will be unique to the child you're mentoring. Nevertheless, both Marynn and I have been pleasantly surprised by our secondary students' keen observations in these conferences. More often than not, our kids already see trends in data. They just need us to either affirm what they know or to ask a few questions to help them fill in the gaps.

Third and finally, teach students to make action plans based on the trends they've noticed. The easiest way to change a habit (or to gain a new one) is to hook what you want to do on to something you're already doing. For weight loss, I replaced soda in the morning with coffee. I swapped green tea for the sodas I usually drank in the afternoon. Over the course of many weeks, I slowly replaced one daily habit with another. Students can do the same. Help yours brainstorm "switches" and "hooks" like I did; switch calling out in class with a secret hand signal or spendable "speaking tickets." Hook reading current news articles to a daily habit of skimming social media on the bus ride home.

Plan to Fail

Willpower is a lot like a muscle. Each of us has only so much, and then we run out. Fortunately, some weaknesses can be avoided through planning. If you know you're likely to run out of willpower, you can plan ahead to solve the problem before it happens. Take for instance my (Marynn's) budgetary woes. After years of effort, it finally occurred to me that I just wasn't successful at tracking credit card purchases. I tried switching to a cash-only system, but that had its own failings (parking garage machines come to mind). After some brainstorming, I decided I needed a credit card that would *stop* letting me spend when I hit a certain limit. One bank visit later, and I was the proud owner of an "allowance" debit card. I started splitting off a small portion of my income and putting it on my allowance card. I can track purchases and the remaining balance using an app. It may sound a bit extreme, but I've heard plenty of folks talk about refusing to buy snack food or candy. By eliminating the temptation, we eliminate the need for willpower.

The challenge is figuring out how to apply that lesson in the classroom. I've got students whose cell phone use is practically insatiable; their best solutions (brainstormed together during conferences) often involve putting their phones in places that are "annoying" to reach, like on top of a bookshelf or in a charging station at the front of the room. Flexible seating offers us similar opportunities for self-regulation conversations. "Which seat will be the most successful for you next marking period and why?" I'll write on the board as a journal or email prompt. Students' entries influence my seating chart decisions in the beginning of the year; towards the end, I allow students to choose their own seats. That privilege comes with the expectation that students will plan to protect themselves from failures of willpower. When I have to draw attention to weak spots, it's never a "gotcha" moment—rather, I pull students aside and ask them to reflect on what isn't working and how we can fix it together. I remind students: eliminate the temptation, and you eliminate the need for willpower.

Willpower Depletion Necessitates Self-Care

Self-care means what it says—caring for yourself. A basic type is when athletes stretch or take ice baths to soothe swollen muscles. We teachers take nutrient supplements to ward off illness. Anything someone does to care for his or her health (physical, emotional, mental, spiritual, etc.) is self-care. It becomes particularly important to invest time and effort in taking care of yourself when your willpower is depleted. Much like lacking sleep, lacking willpower has widespread negative impacts—and, like sleep, willpower can be regained through a simple process of rest and nurture.

My (Cathleen's) grandmother used to say that no one can pour water from an empty cup. When you test your willpower by pushing yourself to be better, you will get worn out. This happens to students using willpower at school, too. Fortunately, there are methods of self-care that work in the classroom. We can teach our students what they are, as well as how and when to use them. Here are a few Marynn and I have found helpful: listening to calming music, visualizing calming scenes, decluttering desks or bookbags, venting to friends, exercising, eating a snack, or drinking cool water. Basically, anything that helps boost a person's mood can help when willpower is depleted. Sometimes it's as simple as knowing when to go take a nap! Students need to know they can always boost their mood and resolve, no matter what situation they find themselves in. Having the language to say, "My willpower is pretty weak right now. Can I take a minute to do some self-care?" may be the difference between a meltdown and a turn around.

Where There's a Will, There's a Way

Willpower is exactly that: power. As teachers, we have the ability to increase willpower in each one of our students. You might nurture the willpower in a future world record breaker, a scientist who helps find a cure for cancer, or a philanthropist who figures out a solution to world hunger. These are only dreams for now. With enough willpower, we can make dreams a reality.

Unlocking Willpower: Big Ideas

Locks:	Keys:
Students don't feel like they have the ability to do something.	Visualization allows students to see their dreams and gives them a purpose that increases their willpower.
Students can feel overwhelmed when they dream big.	Allow students to see that all big dreams and goals need to be broken down into small goals. By allowing students to break their dreams down into a journey of goals it lets them see that their dreams are just a series of steps that need to be accomplished. A mountain looks much less intimidating when there are stairs to the top.
When taking on a big dream or goal students will sometimes get discouraged.	Show students how to use gratitude and positivity to reframe times of struggle in order to keep moving forward.
Students will get tired and have days when they lack the will to try.	Show students ways to take care of themselves when life is overwhelming. Give students tools for self-care to recharge themselves and their will.

So what? We can't change students' home life, and we can't change genetics, but we can teach them to increase their willpower.

Quick Resources for Willpower
1. **A Minute of Gratitude**
   This is a quick activity that works well at the start of class or a week. For exactly one minute have students make a list of all the things they are thankful for in their life. Take the time to point out

small things that may easily be taken for granted, like having food, shelter, and clothing. Have students read over their list at the end of the minute and number the things they are thankful for. This simple tool will help boost students' willpower throughout the day.

2. **One Word: Who Do You Want to Be?**
Instruct students to think for a few minutes about people they admire, from celebrities to friends and family. Then, ask students to list positive characteristics shared by those people. Finally, have students choose some qualities from the list that they want to have when they grow up. Talk students through creating a mental picture of who they want to be some years in the future (imagining themselves on graduation day works well). Have them list positive things their future self is known for or does frequently.

Out of all the traits they've brainstormed, have students choose one to work on. For example, if someone chooses kindness, his goal is to use that characteristic daily until he becomes similar to his vision of his future self. Students should chart their progress towards gaining characteristics. When they reach their personal goal of how often they want to exhibit the characteristic, they can choose another trait to focus on. This way, we are constantly supporting students as they work to become better versions of themselves.

3. **Goal-Planning and Tracking Folder**
Have a folder for students to keep track of their goals and the progress toward their goals. The folder can include pictures for motivation and vision boards for their goals. This folder should serve as motivation for students. When first passing out folders, it's good to have students write their own positive affirmations on the outside of the folder so that just seeing the folder serves as willpower motivation. That way regardless of if it is a bad day on tracking a goal they will have a positive affirmation to pick them up and keep them on the path of progress.

4. **Creating a Self-Care Plan**
At the start of the school year have students make a list of ways they recharge and get more energy. Have students list out ways they have bounced back from failure in the past. Once they have listed all the information have them come up with a plan of things they can do when they are feeling unmotivated or need a break from a challenge. Having a plan in place before students face failure or a setback will help the student know that failure is ok and when it happens they need to take care of themselves so they can get back in the game and keep going.

Reflection on Willpower

A page for you to reflect and write your own thoughts on willpower. Have a great idea or insight? Feel free to share at www.unlockingheroes.com

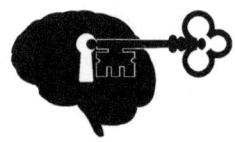

Key Five: Soft Skills

Maiya Kraft—Student
Quirky, gentle, friendly, ebullient
Hero

I started meditating on my own over the summer before 12th grade because it helped me be more in tune with myself. After I became a counselor at summer camp, I had to learn to be a lot more calm in extremely stressful situations. I realized that mindfulness might be able to help. At the camp, we learned about how people think and act, and how we could make sure that the campers were having a good time and being safe. We learned how to understand the campers and how to deal with people around you. I realized when I got home how useful that would be elsewhere. I remembered that as a child, a counselor recommended doing guided imagery when I had a stressful moment. When I got home from camp, I started using meditation to replace guided imagery, and I was amazed at the results. I felt myself becoming a better, happier person.

This fall, I was really shocked when Mrs. Dause started teaching meditation and mindfulness to us in class! I'd never seen anybody at school do mediation before, especially not a teacher, and even more especially not as part of an official class. Having meditation in class twice a week helped me to be less stressed, though. I looked forward to just sitting down and taking a breather for a second to think about what my mind was doing. I could say, "Hey, I'm stressed out, can we take a break?" And we'd all take some mindful breaths and just think about the rest of the day. It helped me to become a more empathetic and organized person.

What Mrs. Dause called SEL helps me most with my peers. It helps me understand how they're feeling. I liked sitting down and learning about it for 15 minutes in the morning. Having that opportunity to not worry about anything else set me up for the rest of the day. It calmed me down and helped me think. I've noticed that my time management actually goes up when I've done meditation or mindfulness. Plus, it's really nice to be able to learn about social-emotional things in school. Those 15-minute lessons gave me back potentially hours because I didn't have to go out and learn the hard way. It saved me so much pain, stress, and time.

I use emotional literacy most among my peers. If my friends come to me with a problem, I have to use emotional literacy to figure out the best way to help them. Where one of my friends might need advice, another friend just needs me to listen and give them a hug. There's a complete difference. I have to really think about it. Having mindfulness, or the ability to sit down and think about how I am, can really help me understand how other people are, too. Things like breathing exercises help me calm down. Even just doing a short breathing exercise at the beginning of the day sets a nice mood. Things like that just help me to be better in general.

After learning all these things, there's an obvious difference in how well I can deal with stressful situations. Now I am able to distance myself and get a better look at what is going on, understand the people around me, and tackle the problem much easier. It leaves me much less stressed and much happier afterward.

Mondays in my (Marynn's) classroom look different than other days of the week. Imagine you've stopped to peer through my window. Here's what you'll see: everyone is sitting in a big circle. A student holds aloft a green foam figurine. The room falls silent while this person speaks. The moment he or she lowers the talking token, the circle erupts in conversation. I sit quietly, my attention shifting from one discussion to another. A copper bell waits in my hand, but I don't ring it yet. The whiteboard glows with a projected document titled "meeting agenda." Some of the words are already obscured by lines and notes scribbled in dry erase marker. This is a typical Monday meeting. It's a collaborative, student-empowered environment, and it's beautiful to watch. But did things always look this way? They most certainly did not! To get here, I had to begin by learning a hard lesson.

At the beginning of my career, I didn't fully realize how impossible it is to do something you've never been taught. Initially, I thought that if I had clear classroom rules and guidelines and stated my expectations in a firm but friendly tone, my high school students would play along with things like "be respectful to yourself and others," "be kind," and "participate." I overlooked one crucial problem: I'd never taken time to find out what my students knew about how to do those things. I assumed they knew what it meant to be respectful and kind; they just chose not to do it sometimes. After all, my kids were 16 and 17 years old. *"They've been in school forever. Of course they know this stuff!"* That assumption led to all sorts of uncomfortable interactions my first couple of years of teaching. I remember one boy in particular who played a large part in showing me exactly how wrong I was.

It was the day of final exams at the end of a long but not particularly difficult class. I felt like I got along well with this young man, but we were about to have our worst conversation of the entire year. Everyone was working steadily, and it took me a few laps around the room to realize that Joel wasn't working at all: his hand was sort of wiggling back and forth on his exam paper, but what he was actually doing was making faces and mouthing silent messages to his friend. They were being sneaky, and I was really frustrated when it dawned on me that they were wasting their limited exam time (not to mention risking distracting all of their classmates). Joel was sitting closest to me, so I walked over and crouched beside his desk. "Hey," I whispered, "You need to knock that off. You can pass this class if you pass this exam, but you're gonna run out of time if you keep goofing off like that. Joel? Joel!"

He wasn't even looking at me. "I hear you, Mrs. Dause. I'm just talkin' to Juwan."

Now I was really mad. "I get that, dude, but what I'm saying is that you can talk to him in a little while … Joel, look at me when I'm talking to you!" And then I did something I've regretted ever since. I snapped my fingers in front of Joel's face. My thought was that if I could break his focus on his friend, he'd cue in to what I was saying. Wrong.

"Do *not* snap in my face!" Suddenly Joel was on his feet, towering over me as I crouched. He was shouting, sweat beading on his forehead. His eyes were wilder than I'd ever seen them. His hands were bunched at his sides, and he was shaking.

Shocked, I tried to salvage the situation. Every kid in the room was looking our way. The drama going down between Joel and me was infinitely more fascinating than the essays they were supposed to be writing. "Whoa, whoa, I'm sorry, Joel, I'm sorry. Sit down. I didn't mean it. I'm sorry. Shhhh, just take a seat. I'm really sorry. I wanted your attention, that's all."

Still shaking, Joel did sit back down, but he looked at me with eyes full of fury and hurt and something I couldn't place. It was like he felt betrayed.

"I was paying attention to you, Mrs. Dause," he muttered quietly. "But I'll be d****d if I'm ever doing that again."

Gut punch. Unsure of what to say, I stood up carefully and sort of backed away. Since Joel was now looking at his paper, the other students' attention drifted back to their work. I thought it was best to let well enough alone, but I was troubled. What had gone wrong? I'd gotten what I wanted, but something felt horribly out of place; I didn't feel successful at all.

I could have avoided this encounter. If I'd taught and used soft skills from the beginning of the semester, the situation could have resolved differently. In all our time together, I never assessed or instructed Joel's class in skills like "communication," "time management," or "emotional intelligence." When I knelt beside Joel's desk that day, I had expectations for his communication skills that I'd never actually taught. Of course we miscommunicated. Joel thought he was paying attention by listening to my words—I thought he was being disrespectful by continuing to look at Juwan while I was talking. In our own minds, we were both right. In practice, our soft skills didn't match up. Joel was a pretty easy-going kid; if I had taken even five minutes to explain what I expected when I needed his attention, he would have done it.

So how do we overcome the very human tendency to react? How do we set our students (not to mention ourselves) up for success? How can we create an innovative classroom community that is going to require them to be good people and to work with others? The answer is simple and complicated: we teach and practice soft skills.

Important Questions

The good news is that you already know how to do this. The application, though, might be new. Here's what we need to ask ourselves about students' soft skills:

> What do they know?
> What do they need?
> How do I teach it?
> Do they know it now, and can they apply it?

And what are those soft skills, exactly? Based on years of classroom experience and a few Google searches, soft skills fall into these eight categories:

Official Skill Name	What It Actually Means
Leadership	Being in charge and making decisions
Communication	Giving and receiving information clearly
Collaboration	Working smoothly with other people
Time management	Getting stuff done without procrastinating to death
Adaptability	Seeking solutions and not freaking out when things go wrong
Critical thinking	Using your brain to analyze, ask, wonder, and create
Emotional intelligence	Mindful self-awareness and self-regulation
Character	Being kind to yourself and others

Here's more good news: most of our kids have some competence with these skills already. For example, if you've ever seen a student break a pencil and then quietly ask around for another one, you've seen native soft skills in play. Every time we ask students to work together to accomplish something, we witness them using soft skills; some kids, of course, have more than others.

In the next few sections, we'll demonstrate what each soft skill looks like in school. We'll also outline how we implement the skills in our classrooms. Some of this may look familiar. If so, you're well on your way to teaching some of the most important skills your students will need to thrive in any situation.

Leadership

Nelson Mandela, George Washington, Mother Teresa, and Steve Jobs were all great leaders, but how did they learn leadership? Not by reading books in a classroom. They learned through experience. Students need to be given the chance to try to solve big problems that may not have answers. They need to leave the classroom and work on something they care about in the world around them. Why? So they can develop courage to take on issues others won't, trust in themselves, and have faith in their ideas and belief in the power of people.

I (Cathleen) have heard it said that leadership cannot be taught. That's true, but Marynn and I believe it can be learned. Much like I can't learn to be a mechanic just by reading a car manual, I can't become a leader by reading a leadership article. However, if I tinker with a car, get input from mechanics, and learn how the car drives from the owner, I may eventually have the skills of a mechanic. Leadership is learned through experience and laying a foundation. Students need to learn the key components (communication, mediation, and courage) and test them out by putting them into action.

One of the greatest things we can do for our students to help foster leadership is trust them enough to take on real problems that matter. Every summer, I go around the community and ask if various groups need help or if they have problems that need solving. When I visit, my question usually gets stares of disbelief or raised eyebrows, especially when I tell them I have future leaders of the world who want to help. "My goal," I say, "is to produce leaders like the ones you have in your organization. In order to do that, my students need to learn by working beside and with people who are already leaders. So, how can we help you?" I explain that I'll present all of the challenges to my students, who will choose one to work on for the year. Once I've collected all of the ideas and problem-solving opportunities, I present the list to my students. Then they choose issues to tackle. Every community is unique. Even if you can't find problems to solve locally, there are educators and issues that are just a click away if you search for them. One of the things I've heard said constantly is that we are educating children for jobs and problems that don't yet exist. That may be the case. If we are going to raise bold leaders who look fearlessly into the unknown, we have to give them the chance to hone their leadership skills against problems that exist today.

> **Tip for Teacher Heroes**
>
> This process of finding challenges in your local area for students to work on can be intimidating, to say the least. Start small. Look close to your school building. Is there someone you can try to encourage? Are there places that need special attention or care? How can you leverage what's right in front of you to bring the world to your students? Start there. Then you can begin (slowly) growing outward.

Communication

Because communication is the process of transmitting and receiving information, my (Marynn's) classes learn it through play. I find that classic team-building games from summer camp work well as object studies for communication skills. For example, I might challenge students to guide a blindfolded teammate along a simple course using only words, sounds, or tugs on a guiding rope. In a reflection discussion afterwards, "followers" always have strong opinions about right and wrong ways to communicate directions! Active listening is a skill that students have frequently never heard of. After a few games, discussion practices, and a video or two, though, every one of them can list descriptors of good active listening: "undivided attention," "eye contact," "on-topic responses," and "reflecting or mirroring your partner's words and attitude" always come up.

I also demonstrate qualities of good communication by comparing two versions of the same project description or doing a short role-play skit. Students and I work together to write a list describing what good communication looks like. I bring the list back out for Monday meetings and whenever we're doing group work. Communication is a soft skill that is easy to teach but hard to master. That's why we practice, reflect, and practice again all year long!

Collaboration

Collaboration is communication's big brother. Once students have learned the basics of good communication skills, they can begin learning how to collaborate well. The biggest key here is giving students structures to follow and "look fors" to help them stay on track in the beginning. For example, team jobs or table roles are a good way to start kids off. I find that jobs and roles aren't something to use indefinitely—if I stick with the same ones for too long, the defined "responsibilities" get restrictive, crushing creativity and initiative. As introductory structures and occasional activity tools, though, team jobs work well.

Another important aspect is involving students in listing "look fors" before working together. Even the youngest students can be quite successful at this, provided their teachers support and guide the conversation. With older children, I like to have pairs or small groups brainstorm lists of describing words for "good collaboration/teamwork." Then, students send up representatives to write their top three to five ideas on the whiteboard for everyone to see. Once everyone's seated again, I lead a search for categories. I draw lines between words with similar meanings, write category titles, and eventually end up with a short list that students copy into their notebooks. That list may also end up posted in our classroom as an anchor chart; hello, bulletin board décor!

Reflection is the last step in teaching collaboration. It's also the most important. Collaboration changes with every partner, team, and group. To be successful, students must practice accurately assessing their own participation as well as the group's workflow. And it does take practice; how many kids do you know who are entirely objective about their own words and actions? With a steady, repeated process of self and group assessment, though, children can develop this key trait. Conferences with the teacher round out the exercise. Once groups have self- and peer-assessed their collaboration efforts, find time to review the results with them, even if only for a minute or two. The key to teaching this skill, like anything, is structured feedback and repetition.

> **Tip for Teacher Heroes**
>
> Don't be surprised if you get a bit of push back from students on the process of self-reflection. I've found that my learners are frequently much more enthusiastic about reviewing *other* people's contributions than they are their own. The best solution I've found is to share my own self-reflections after teaching tough lessons or trying new things. This is very much a lead-by-example situation.

Time Management

When it comes to teaching time management, we teachers are great at giving students practice with projects and due dates. Too often, though, we leave out the part our kids don't know—how to balance time for the demands of life and school! When I (Cathleen) was in school, one of the hardest things I had to learn on my own was figuring out how to get everything done. No one bothered to teach me time management. I eventually learned it, but imagine if someone had shown me how to prioritize and design my day. The gift of time management would have allowed me to optimize my time, feel less stressed, and discover a critical school–life balance. Kids need the opportunity to use backwards design to set manageable project goals. Time management is a skill we need to guide students through multiple times. Like the rest of us, kids learn what works for them through trial and error.

At the start of the school year, I like to have students write about heroes in their lives and present a speech at a banquet. When I initially assign the task, I hand students a blank sheet of paper and walk them through how to plan to complete the project on time. First, students break down the project into all of its component tasks. Next, I have them estimate the amount of time each task will take to complete based on prior experience. Last, I show the schedule of work days students will have for the project. Students set attainable goals for themselves based on their time estimates. No two planning papers are ever the same because each student has different activities and responsibilities. Students gain ownership and a better perspective of their working habits when they experience forming a plan to use time management. This also prepares kids to be successful in their future professional lives.

Adaptability

Adaptability means facing problems, changes, and unexpected scenarios head on … without losing your cool. We teachers use it all the time. But how do we teach it? Just like all of the other soft skills, adaptability is taught best through an unequal combination of direct instruction and experience. I say unequal because it's 100% possible to say too much when trying to explain it. For most students, about three to five minutes of verbal description is plenty for them to get the gist of what adaptability looks like. Telling stories is a good place to start. Referencing public acts of adaptation is even better, and you get the best of both worlds if you can tell a story about a local person (maybe even a student!) whose adaptation skills led to success. Tie the lesson to students' lives. "Remember Friday's football game," I might say, "when the quarterback's play fell apart? Remember how he just took off running, and then he found someone to pass to? That was adaptability!" Bam, they get it.

The one other thing to toss out there before sending students off to learn experientially is this—adaptability breaks down into three parts: behaviors, thoughts, and emotions. It's wise to help students learn to look at each of the parts before trying to combine them as a whole. In the football story, for example, most students could pretty easily distinguish the quarterback's behavioral, intellectual, and emotional responses to having his play ruined. You can repeat the exercise with another, more difficult example—perhaps a video or news clip about a regular Joe who adapted to drastic, unexpected change. This kind of observation and analysis can be done briefly, say on a sticky note, or in long form. The important thing is to help students practice seeing each part of the overall reaction.

Finally, students are eventually going to need the chance to experience adaptability for themselves. The traditional school day involves a lot of changes (class to class, teacher to teacher, subject to subject, etc.). Nevertheless, when you're teaching adaptability itself, students benefit most from specific, intentional practice. Try playing a game and then changing the rules in the middle of it. Offer opportunities to go new places and interact with new people: visiting other classes or schools, going on field trips, hosting visitors in your room, and social learning sites like FlipGrid.com are all excellent opportunities. Lead students in reflection after each experience. "How did my behavior change? What did I think when ____? Which emotions did I notice? What did I do well, and how could I do better next time?" Practice doesn't happen in a vacuum, of course. For most of my classes, we learn about adaptability while posting FlipGrid videos about passion projects and reading goals that aren't going according to plan.

Speaking of not going to plan, the hardest part of adaptability is usually the fear response. Adjusting to change is hard. It sucks. Especially when things change unexpectedly, it's natural to panic a little bit. Owning that discomfort is part of teaching adaptability, too. Be honest with your students when challenges arise in their classroom, school, or community. Talk about how hard things affect you and how you're adjusting your response. Help students work through coping strategies and tools that will empower them to choose their own responses. Here are a few good ones:

- Prevent yourself from immediately reacting. When stressed or scared, take three deep breaths before acting.
- Have a plan A, but have fallbacks, too. Think through what you'll do in "uh oh" to "worst case" scenarios—plans B, C, D, and so on.
- Always have an exit strategy. It's very rare to find yourself in a situation where you can't walk away. With the exception of true emergencies, you can always choose when, where, and how to respond.

Perhaps you can see, dear reader, how skills like these will benefit your students. You may even have in mind a child (or three) who could benefit from discussions like these. Be encouraged! By spending just a few minutes with those students, you can highlight what they're already learning. "Hey, guys," you might say. "I was just thinking about how adaptable you're being right now …" It isn't a new lesson. It's not even a bullet point in your plan for the day. Teaching soft skills is like a secret weapon or favorite tool you can use when the moment calls for it. Open your students' eyes to the adaptability they're using every day, and you will grow learners who can cope better, have a stronger basis for self-control, and adjust to changes more smoothly than ever before.

Critical Thinking

Critical thinking is forming opinions and drawing conclusions independently. Students are natural critical thinkers. It's easy to overlook that skill, however, because we give children lots of content knowledge without enough time to think about how it fits into their understanding of the world. We can begin to nurture students' natural skill set by promoting curiosity. Encourage students to delve into content by asking questions with no clear answers. Intentionally cultivate a classroom full of inquiring questioners.

A simple tool I (Cathleen) use to promote critical thinking is a "parking lot"—this is a big sheet of paper that's stocked with sticky notes and pencils. I tell students to "park" their thoughts and questions there during class. As the day continues, other kids and I go by and answer posted questions or add on to chains of thoughts. By giving students a space that promotes free thinking, my learners freely explore the concepts they are learning.

Another tool that really promotes critical thinking is debate—an oldie but a goodie! Give students an open-ended problem or concept. Show them how to explore both sides of the issue. Consider using structures like a Lincoln–Douglas debate format where participants find out their "side" on debate day itself! (I do occasionally allow my students to pick sides ahead of time, but only after they've researched the arguments for and against.) It's amazing to watch students question content, sources, and one other as they try to form opinions and draw conclusions. Critical thinking with debate promotes mutual understanding, too. It shows students that even though they might not agree, they can still work together and be friends despite having different worldviews.

> **Tip for Teacher Heroes**
>
> Classwide debates for building social-emotional skills? Yes! But it only works if you front-load the process with lessons on mutual respect, polite disagreement, and "accountable talk moves." I particularly emphasize brainstorming sentence stems and conversation look fors with students before we do any kind of structured discussions (or debates) as a class.

Emotional Intelligence

I (Marynn) began teaching emotional intelligence in sort of a backwards way. Being a person with a powerful temper myself, I know what it's like to get angry at your teammates. That's why it struck a chord with me when I heard a counselor say, "Anger is defensive. It always stems from unmet needs." It makes sense. Why do babies scream and rage? They have a need, right? And what makes middle-schoolers the angriest? Usually the unmet need to fit in with and be accepted by their peers. Why are children from hard places so often angry? Their deepest need, for safety, isn't being met. The list goes on.

That being the case, I began emotional intelligence lessons by hosting conflict resolution workshops with my students. I took the idea my counselor had shared and multiplied it out. Any time student partners, teammates, or group members would come to me frustrated with one another, I'd start asking questions. "You know," I told them. "Psychologists say that anger is really just needs that aren't being met. So, what do you need? How can you meet someone else's need? What do you need from me?" And off we'd go, taking turns answering each question. I took notes on scratch paper. If needed, I steered the conversation back around to a need I'd heard not be met yet. "Bobby, Angel said that to feel confident about this project, she needs to know the group is getting things done on time. Jacey and Samantha have already had their turns, and they've got great ways they're going to help meet your need and each other's. How can you help Angel know the group is getting things done on time?" With a little prompting and a *lot* of reflecting back to students what they'd said, I learned that nearly all of my students really did want to get along—they simply didn't know how to do it under pressure.

A few years after beginning my ad hoc conflict resolution workshops, I started learning about mindfulness and self-regulation. (Attending adoption classes for my son had a lot to do with this.) Mindfulness, in essence, is the ability to pay attention to what's happening in your own head without getting overwhelmed or carried away by it. Similarly, self-regulation is the ability to recognize and take care of your own needs so you can control your emotional reactions. Both are powerhouse skills for students to master. Fortunately, they can be taught with little to no materials. Sometimes preparation goes by the wayside, too! I frequently model these skills by calling attention to how I'm feeling and responding or how a student is doing so. Since my classes practice mindfulness together using recordings on Headspace.com twice weekly, we have natural discussion points built into our routine. For example, after practicing, I often take a moment to think aloud about things I noticed in my own thoughts. "Today I felt really sad and tired," I might say. "It feels like today is going to last forever, but I know from past experience that it won't. So I'm going to drink extra water and maybe eat a little chocolate, and I'm really going to focus on how much fun it is for me to spend time with you all. That will help me feel a little better and be able to enjoy this day even though I don't feel so good."

These kinds of guided observations make for great student journaling prompts in my language arts classes. Even without writing, though, there are plenty of ways for students to practice being mindful of their emotions and self-regulating. Two of our favorites are activities called "rank it" and "roses and thorns," which I'll explain in more detail in the Quick Activities section at the end of this chapter.

Character

I (Cathleen) have seen teachers chastise students for forgetting to use a character trait that was taught in the classroom. The honest truth is that we all mess up, and it's impossible to expect someone to always be at their best. We all fall short. The focus of teaching character is helping kids do the right thing in times of trial. After all, true character becomes evident when problems arise. Grandma used to say, "The mirror of life reveals your character because it's forged by fire, fear, and fake people."

Students need time to work on character traits in school. One good way to do this is role-playing scenarios and conversations. Stories highlighting positive character traits, like ones in *The Book of Virtues: A Treasury of Great Moral Stories* by William J. Bennett, can be used as models. However, students also need to be taught that adhering to these character traits is a lofty goal; it's not going to be possible all the time. I don't know about you, but I make some kind of character trait misstep every day! Be it getting irrationally irritated, forgetting something, or failing to fulfill a promise, I'm always in the process of messing up and trying again. We teachers need to be honest in sharing times we've stumbled in the face of failure. By demonstrating the process of admitting mistakes and working to get back on track, we lead through example. It's the most powerful way to instill character lessons in students as well as our own families.

Students should also have time to look at the character failures and successes of people throughout history. (I particularly recommend the book *How They Choked: Failures, Flops, and Flaws of the Awfully Famous* by Georgia Bragg.) It's one thing to role-play what good character traits look like in practice, but it's another to see how real people tried to implement them and "choked." Students can use these stories to talk, discuss, and imagine what they would do in similar situations. In these conversations, teachers can emphasize resilience. History's greatest heroes achieved victory because they didn't give up in the face of moral failure. Students are bound to succeed when they know they can always try again.

Takeaway

When we teach students soft skills, we're inviting them to problem solve. After all, that's what heroes do best. Few superheroes go running to their masters when difficulties arise. If they did, we wouldn't recognize them as heroes. What would we call those needy, dependent characters? Children? *Students*? I propose that we've left our learners in that role for too long. Students can become masters; in fact, that is their purpose.

Unlocking Soft Skills: Big Ideas

Locks:	Keys:
Teachers expect students to "just know" how to behave.	Students need a chance to explicitly learn and develop soft skills in class. They need time to reflect and develop goals for deeper personal growth.
Students are told to be leaders but are given roles managing peers instead of leading them.	True leadership is developed by serving and helping the people you lead. Students need help learning how to do this.
Students confuse having the ability to speak with knowing how to communicate clearly.	Students learn adaptive, flexible communication skills by interacting with different people and learning from others.
Teachers expect students to figure out how to manage project work and timelines.	Students learn time management skills when teachers model backwards design and help students create action plans.
Teachers assume students know how to adapt to changes.	Students need to be taught not just how to cope, but how to thrive in a changing environment. They need a chance to figure out their natural adaptive skills and to learn coping strategies for weaknesses.

🔒 Teachers think puzzles and comprehension questions teach critical thinking.	🗝 Students need to practice thinking critically about real-world problems. This involves looking at each problem through different lenses and seeking a variety of perspectives.
🔒 Students and teachers tend to think of emotions as "only for counselors."	🗝 Students need to be shown how to recognize, name, and appropriately handle what they're feeling both in and out of the classroom.
🔒 Teachers become frustrated when students don't implement character traits after they've been taught.	🗝 Character traits should be taught, studied, and modeled daily. However, teachers also need to model resilience. Everyone messes up, but we can start again at any moment.

So what? By teaching soft skills, we strengthen students' abilities to build human connections. This will forever impact children's jobs, relationships, and overall well-being.

Quick Activities for Soft Skills

1. **Create a Problem Bank**
   Remember that all problems are just opportunities for students to flex their SEL muscles and do service learning. Have students generate a list of ideas of problems in the community. Then, go out in the community and ask organizations for problems or tasks they need help with. Put the problems into a spreadsheet and share it with students. Invite students to tackle the problems they feel the most connected to. Also, check out books like *Start Now! You Can Make a Difference* by Chelsea Clinton; it lists local non-profit organizations you can connect and work with. The more problems in your bank, the more opportunities you have to give your students real-world learning experiences. You'll learn more about this in the "Service" chapter!
2. **Class Meetings**
   Once a week or so, set aside 10–15 minutes. Label it "Class Meeting." Write a simple meeting agenda where students can see it. My schedule looks like this:
   a) **Greeting**
   b) **Check in**: "How is everyone doing?" or "Rank it!"
   c) **Housekeeping**: basic school-wide announcements and paperwork
   d) **Question**: "I need your help figuring out ____"

or "What do you think about ____?"
or "We could do ___ or ___. Which would you prefer and why?"
   e) **Upcoming events**: things we're doing next and why students will benefit
      ♦ Sometimes I also use this time to share unit-planning decisions with students. For example, "We have a summative assessment coming up. I could give you a test, or we could try a review poster project. I'd appreciate your input while I make my decision. Please write your comments on a sticky note and drop them in the class basket for me."
3. **Role Play/Games**
   Tap into students' childhood experiences of playing pretend; although I've demonstrated how to do a role-play in class, I've never yet had to teach learners how to pretend to be someone else! Set up a scenario that serves your teaching purpose and is easy to envision. Here are two examples:
   ♦ **Realistic scenario**: Your friend is upset after receiving a message and you want to help, but he's really private and doesn't like opening up. What can you say to be supportive while respecting his boundaries?
   ♦ **Silly and unrealistic**: You've finished building the engine for your spacecraft, and your classmate wants to borrow it for a space race. You know the rules say racers are supposed to build their own engines. How can you firmly but kindly tell her "no?"
4. **Mindfulness Activities: "Rank It" and "Roses and Thorns"**
   For "Rank It," teacher and students "rank" their day using the fingers on one hand. A hand with five fingers represents "what a great day!" and one finger means "this day has been awful." Let students help you define what the other three options mean. Ring a bell or use another signal to begin the activity. At the sound, everyone holds up a hand "ranking" their day. Encourage students to look around at their neighbors. Take special note of folks whose days are down at one and two fingers. They'll probably need some extra encouragement.

   "Roses and Thorns" is another name for "Highs and Lows." I have my students stand in a big circle. We go around quickly saying one thing that's good in our lives (the rose), and one thing that's hard or uncomfortable (the thorn). The script looks like this: "Rose, _____. Thorn, _____." Everyone listening is invited to snap or nod when they hear things they agree or can empathize with. Should anyone wish not to participate, the alternate script is just to wave and say, "Good morning!" The rest of the circle waves

and says "Good morning!" in return.For classes that don't do well standing still and waiting in big circles, I've done variations. A few ideas:
- Share roses and thorns in pairs
- Share in trios or quadruplets and have one randomly selected speaker report to the class what a group mate said
- Work in small groups to write each other's roses and thorns with dry erase marker on laminated pictures of actual roses with thorns
    - Those make a nice whiteboard display for the day. It's interesting to see everyone's highs and lows all at once!

5. **Class Debate**

First, show students a list of age-appropriate topics. Allow them a chance to vote on the topic. Having a high-interest topic will increase engagement and help kids invest more energy in doing the preparation work for the debate. Allow students time to research their topic and present their findings. There are many different formats you can use. Try a variety of styles and formats. I like using a ball to clearly show whose turn it is to talk. Using debate allows kids to use critical thinking and communication, as well as collaboration if they work in teams.

Further resources: visit our website at www.unlockingheroes.com

Reflection on Soft Skills

A page for you to reflect and write your own thoughts on soft skills. Have a great idea or insight? Feel free to share at www.unlockingheroes.com

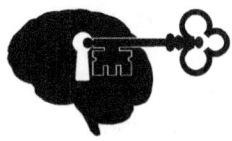

Key Six: Service

Maia MacMahon—Student
Activist, sarcastic, Girl Scout, bibliophile,
Hero

At school, most of what we do is take notes, do homework, and prepare for tests. After many years in the school system, I'd come to accept that. But one day, it all changed.

I was your average honors student, and I knew how school "worked." I sat down on the first day of eighth grade in my third-period English class, thinking I knew what to expect. Then Mrs. Beachboard stood up at the front of the room.

"This is not your normal English class," she said. "You see that?" She pointed to the word "Heroes" that was painted on the door. "That's not just some word meant to inspire students. In here, we are heroes." Ok, I thought this seems interesting. "Before school started, I went around town and asked people if they had problems. I had them write them on little pieces of paper, and we're going to try to solve these problems." We looked at each other. Either she was crazy, or she was awesome. We were leaning towards the latter. Sadly, the bell rang, and class was over.

Over the next few weeks, my class decided to help the Department of Social Services (DSS). We discovered that their domestic violence unit needed help with funding and raising awareness around the county. To help solve the problem, we decided to help DSS create a family-friendly celebration for the community. We combined forces with DSS and started having weekly planning meetings. Back in the classroom, we got together in groups and wrote, produced, directed, edited, and starred in public service announcements and ads to get the word out. Everyone had a blast. Then came October, the month of the event.

With October came a massive rush of things that had to be done. We had to make capes for the workers to wear, organize and order a lot of decorations, and post about the event on all forms of social media. We also needed to get sponsors to fund the activities. One Saturday before the event, a group of us went with Mrs. Beachboard to Main Street to ask local businesses to help. The first business we went into was a jewelry store; the owner came running out after us and gave us a check for $100. He started talking to us, and then he gave us his business card, which read Carter Nevill, Mayor. I couldn't believe that the mayor supported our mission!

On the day of the event, we arrived early to add finishing touches on the decorations and help the vendors set up. After four nerve-racking hours, our event officially opened to the public. I stood behind a table making balloon animals (which I learned how to do in class) while my friends helped out at other stations.

Eventually, the flow of people in the children's gym slowed to a crawl. Most of us workers ended up on the floor, playing with a few of the little kids. But even as the evening came to an end, we all felt amazing. For the first time in our school lives, we felt like we had been a part of something major. We had solved a problem for the community, raised funds, and even gotten computers donated to the DSS. We felt important, even powerful in a way. In the timespan of a few months, we learned we didn't need to wait to be adults to change the world. In short, we learned we have the power in us every day to choose to be heroes.

Service. The concept might seem old and worn out, but it's the heart of my (Cathleen's) classroom. From a young age, my parents taught me that people matter more than anything. I remember one particular November when my mother let us know we were going to have a second "Thanksgiving" dinner. We were hosting this dinner especially for a resident from the nursing home where Mom worked. I was more than ok with extra pies and turkey, but I didn't understand why. With just a few words, my mother inspired me that night. Her belief became my cornerstone for empowering students.

I walked up to my mom while she stood over the sink doing dishes.

"Mom, I'm cool with second Thanksgiving, but, ummm … Why can't you just drop a meal off to this lady?"

My mother stopped what she was doing and wiped her hands on a towel. She turned, her face scrunched and irritated.

"Cathleen." *She used my full name, not my nickname*, I thought, *Uh oh.* "You have a family, a connection with support," Mom continued. "We sit down to dinner all together to connect with you. It's less about the meal and more about being together. If we dropped off a meal to this woman, she would get the food, but not the warming comfort of fellowship. People need people; it's as natural as your need to breathe air. Serving others teaches us who we are and what it means to be human. Money, jobs, and things come and go, but serving others is the greatest life instructor. Purpose and passion show up when you help people."

Later that day, we had a beautiful meal laughing and smiling with our elderly guest. I told bad jokes, my brother made disgusting fart noises, and my parents provided casual small talk. It only took an hour.

As my mom went to get the woman's coat, I sat with her in the living room. She smiled at me. My insides lit up like the fourth of July. She took my hand with feeble fingers and said, "Your mom is a good woman. Today was the best day I have had in a long time."

I felt amazing sitting there with her. At the time, I thought it was because of the great desserts. Years later, I would realize it was the warmth of our connection.

No matter how diverse people are, we all share one purpose: helping each other. From custodians to entrepreneurs, line cooks to judges, all jobs on this planet share the foundation of serving people. Custodians help keep environments clean so people can stay healthy. Entrepreneurs come up with new ideas, ways, and businesses to improve lives (ok, and also to make money). Line cooks provide food to nourish customers. Service is a basic component of the purpose of every person's job. It's a tendency so ingrained in our DNA that helping others actually gives us a boost of "happy hormones," including dopamine, serotonin, and oxytocin.

Here's the fascinating thing: those same "happy hormone" chemicals are essential to learning. Consider how learning involves curiosity, risk taking, and failure. Every one of those comes with risk attached. Kids are naturally scared of failure. Even though we learn from failure, it never feels good. Fear activates our survival instinct of "fight, flight, or freeze." In order to overcome fear, particularly of failure, students need courage. But there's good news! We can embolden our students with a shot of biological courage through service learning. In his article "The Neurochemicals of Happiness" in *Psychology Today*, author Christopher Bergland calls serotonin "the confidence molecule." The more serotonin a person has, the more courageous he will be. The key to getting kids to take risks in learning is built into their DNA, and we need to access it! Service learning provides all the great benefits of service and allows us to teach content as a tool for students to help others.

Service Learning vs. Volunteering

There is a big difference between volunteering and service learning, though. As a student in high school and college, I (Marynn) had many wonderful opportunities to volunteer. I refereed youth soccer games, collected canned goods for battered women's shelters, and tutored underprivileged elementary scholars in after-school programs. These experiences were fun and fulfilling. Participating in them was optional—you might even say voluntary! I did them because I wanted to. (The fact that they looked good on a college résumé didn't hurt, either.)

Service learning takes the best elements of volunteering and combines them with the tenets of problem or project-based learning. With service learning, students learn content knowledge by doing or creating something to serve others. For example:

- A choir class might learn a capella vocal harmonies by practicing to go caroling.
- Science students can learn about filtration and biosystems by cleaning local ponds.
- History and social studies students can research original sources and proper citation methods by building local museum displays or helping at local archaeological sites.
- Learners in Math classes might help libraries, nonprofits, or even individual citizens solve "number problems" by estimating replacement needs, generating fundraising plans, or proposing household budgets and investment strategies.

> **Tip for Teacher Heroes**
>
> Are arguments and excuses racing through your head right now, friend? They did that to me, too. I knew service learning was a well-respected, thoroughly proven method of teaching (with a long history, to boot!). I knew it would probably be good for my kids. It just felt so ... *not my job*. Too big. Too hard. Too unusual, in my original school. All those negatives are real and valid. But so is this: getting into service learning saved my motivation to teach. Maybe it will do the same for you.

In all of these scenarios, students must acquire content knowledge in order to be successful. Their motivation for learning, however, is centered on the desire to serve. It's a purpose nearly everyone is born with. How many times have mothers of toddlers despaired over their children's wholehearted attempts "to help"? Service learning connects a natural longing to the task of learning.

Questioning Success

In the world of education, we usually measure learning with metrics. According to most standard metrics, if a student gets 100% on a test, achieves honor roll, and graduates with honors, he is successful. There are many people who are successful according to society's metrics of wealth, fame, money, and power. Nevertheless, you and I both know that model students and working adults can "have it all" and still be miserable. The hospice patients Bronnie Ware interviewed (see preface) led lives full of success according to society, but they were filled with regret. Why? "Success" without fulfillment is failure.

Obviously, we want our students to find both success and fulfillment. Doing this will require us to broaden our focus. Instead of looking just at finite content metrics, we're going to have to help students expand their view of education. Kids who would normally learn for the purpose of passing a test will have to shift their priorities. Initially, this may be difficult. There is no hard and fast metric for service. The learning students gain while serving can be measured, but "how well did I serve?" has infinite possibilities.

Service learning lets students contribute to something bigger than they may have ever imagined. Seeing that they matter and are needed changes kids' perspective. They begin to see fulfillment and success beyond their possessions and/or percentage scores. Giving kids a purpose for learning that's bigger than themselves sparks passion. It might just lead them to live successfully with no regrets.

Begin with Problems

To create authentic learning and help the world, begin with problems. In the last chapter, we mentioned the creation of a problem bank to help build soft skills. That's because service learning allows kids to practice soft skills, find fulfillment in success, and learn content all at once. Collecting problems is like throwing darts at your curriculum—the more problems you have, the more opportunities to hit your targets.

After introducing students to the problems you've collected, allow them to investigate and add to the bank. You can always go back and figure out curriculum tie-ins for new issues as they're suggested. When students explore problems, they become informed citizens who don't shy away from difficult situations. You'll probably never have time to tackle everything on the list. Still, the simple act of recognizing and considering solutions sets the precedent that all problems are just solutions waiting to happen.

Organization and Planning

When I (Marynn) started experimenting with service learning, I quickly realized I needed to plan in ways I hadn't before. I was used to working in this order: content, skill, practice, and then assessment. For my students to write stories based on the oral histories of nursing home residents, though, we were going to have to do things differently.

Through trial and error, I learned that my job as the teacher was to figure out the big picture. What were my kids going to have to do in order to accomplish their mission? In what order? Then, I planned content knowledge and skill lessons based on what they would need for each step. For our oral history and story-writing mission, my students needed interview skills before they needed to know about plot arcs. Although I felt uncomfortable because the whole thing worked backwards from the way I was used to teaching narratives, it fit the task. What's more, my recalcitrant, reluctant students bloomed. At our first meeting with the nursing home residents, kids who'd made names for themselves as big and bad shrank against the walls, overcome with nerves. Students I'd known as wallflowers took the lead and used their listening skills to connect with our senior interviewees. By the third meeting, elders and students alike greeted one another like old friends. Plus, the entire class turned in the best writings they'd done all semester. Those victories absolutely made up for my discomfort during planning, and then some.

Over time, I've honed my technique. Now, I present a list of options to my students during a class meeting at the beginning of each unit. "Here's what we need to learn," I say. "And here are four ways we could do it. Please help me decide which one we should do." Students point out pros and cons of each option, and then we put it to a vote. I'm careful only to share options I'm certain will serve to fulfill our content learning goals, and I always have at least the outline of a plan in mind for each one before sharing with students.

Once we've made the decision together, though, it's time for students to pitch in on the planning process. I teach all of my learners how to "backwards design" early in the semester. When it comes time to plan a unit, they have the tools necessary for success. "What's our end goal?" I ask. "We have x amount of time to work. What steps do we need to follow? When will we need to finish each one?" Acting as the so-called "guide on the side," I walk my students through the process of planning out a timeline to achieve the mission they've selected. As my friend Todd Finley, Ph.D., says, I'm always careful to explain "things I can't or am not willing to alter" as needed. My job as teacher is to establish a delicate balance between respecting students as colleagues and leading firmly to ensure what they plan is both practical and content-aligned.

Reflection

Another aspect of service learning that separates it from volunteering is intentional reflection. This means guiding students through the process of reviewing their actions and realizations. These are the questions I always use to begin teaching reflection:

- What happened?
- What went well?
- What could have been better?
- How can you improve next time?

Reflecting throughout service learning is important because it gives students time to condense, organize, and store things they're discovering. Remember the dual purpose of service learning: to learn content knowledge while doing good for others. It can be an overwhelming experience for some learners, especially if they've never done anything like it before. To slow and structure the making of memory, help students build a habit of reflection.

Because reflection uses language to encode learning from experience, it can be done using nearly any kind of speaking, writing, reading, or listening. Plan to take frequent reflection breaks with your students. At the beginning, it's particularly important to provide a concrete structure. My students respond well to 3-2-1 style prompts like this: "Describe three things you observed while working today. Explain two challenges you faced. Name one thing you're looking forward to about continuing our work tomorrow." You can also experiment with broader questions and thinking tasks. "Write a letter to yourself in a month explaining what you're doing right now and what you've learned from it. Ask your future self questions about how this activity turns out." Text messages, social media, and peer discussions can also be powerful avenues of reflection. Play around with the communication tools available to you and your scholars.

Find ways to encourage (and yes, even require) students to think backwards and forwards about their work. Emphasize through your questions what they're learning about the course content, but beware—sometimes students don't think they're learning "school stuff"! Be prepared to ask probing, leading questions to help them get at the heart of what they're discovering. In our oral history project, for example, many of my students balked at the idea that they were learning anything about storytelling. "He didn't say anything that can be a story, Mrs. Dause!" they'd protest. "All he talked about was falling off a ladder and breaking his back and then learning to walk again!" Bingo. That was my cue to begin talking about conflict, climax, and character development through difficulties. A few minutes later, those same students' eyes were aglow. "Oh! So like the fall and learning to walk … that *was* his story? Ok, wait, we've got to start writing." Light bulb.

> **Tip for Teacher Heroes**
>
> Heads up! Reflection is easy to overlook. In the heat of the moment, with timelines tangled and seven kids yelling your name at once, it's super easy to just ditch the reflection part of today's lesson. Don't do it. Whatever else you have to cut, keep reflection in the process. Give guiding questions. Engage with students who seem confused or downtrodden. This is where the learning cements—you're going to want to be there when it happens!

I learned (from failure!) the importance of stopping students to reflect at each stage of service learning. If you wait too long to reflect, pieces of students' newly gained knowledge begin to fall through the cracks. A single reflection at the end of a big unit or project will almost always result in shallow, glossed-over thinking. To capture everything they're learning, students need time to reflect after completing each step. One of the easiest ways to track student reflections is through journals or blogs. Students' writing can help you gauge their understanding of content. It also allows you to provide coaching and micro-lessons as needed.

Demonstration

If reflections are rest stops on the journey of service learning, the final destination is demonstration and celebration. A demonstration captures the entire service learning experience: problem, preparation, curriculum, actions, and results. It's an opportunity for students to showcase and celebrate their learning with everyone who was involved in the service learning: participants, helpers, family, and community members.

In my (Cathleen's) classroom, we use two types of service learning demonstration: project presentations and community fairs. For project presentations, students share results with their families and anyone else who was involved in their service learning. Scholars have the opportunity to connect with the people by sharing the personal impact of their projects. For example, at the end of our attempt to get the division's school budget passed, my students chose to speak at a Board of Supervisors meeting. During the public comment section of the meeting, 26 students took turns explaining what they'd learned while running a public awareness campaign about the upcoming vote. They encouraged audience members to ask the Board to fund the budget. When they sat down, the audience burst into applause. Everyone present that night witnessed middle school students using their knowledge for a greater purpose. It was a great culminating demonstration of learning.

We've also hosted giant community fairs as demonstrations of learning. One of those was a county-wide literacy fair. This year, my students worked with the DSS to put on a community awareness day. Students worked all day at the fair. Then at the end, students, parents, attendees, and social workers gathered in the gym for a closing ceremony. Students delivered brief speeches to me summarizing what they'd learned. They made plans to continue serving with the DSS. Many parents were amazed by what their children had accomplished. The ceremony ended with my students surrounding their social worker collaborators and friends with a giant group hug.

A Bridge to Citizenship

By helping the DSS, my students took a problem and used it as an opportunity to make a difference. Service learning models how to be an active participant in the world. It shows learners that nothing gets better instantly, but taking the time to start is the first step to real change.

The greatest thing about service learning? By being out and about in the community, students see the unwritten obligation of each member to assist as they can and where they're needed. This is citizenship in action. When a large group comes together and acts, students see how people are stronger together. Children need not sit back and wait for a hero to save the day; they can begin the good work themselves.

Takeaway

When Marynn and I were coming up with titles for this book, we agreed to use the word "hero." Most people associate the word "hero" with strength and power. Interestingly, "hero" comes from the Proto-Indo-European root "*ser-*." It's one of the sources for our English word "service." The words "hero" and "service" share the same ancient root. Heroes serve a greater cause. By serving others, heroes discover their own strength, ability, and purpose. We humans are born with the biological drive to help one another. It's in our nature. In short, our students were made to be heroes.

Unlocking Service: Big Ideas

Locks:	Keys:
Students are apathetic and don't care to learn.	Students are biologically programmed to feel good when helping others. If we want to help our kids get motivated, we need to give them a reason.
My students volunteer outside of school, so there is no need for service learning.	Volunteering and service learning are not the same thing. Students need their teacher to guide them to access course content they can use to make a difference in the community.
My students are already successful, so I don't need service learning.	Success is fleeting. A student can have a perfect GPA but no fulfillment. Success without fulfillment is still failure.
Service learning sounds like a lot of work I don't have time for.	By going out in the community and making connections, we gain valuable relationships and connections to help our classrooms. Use your village to help your students grow!

So what? Service learning offers students the opportunity to fulfill their biological desire to help and teaches them how to be responsible, caring, participating members of society.

Quick Resources for Service

The resources in this chapter can connect you with outside organizations to begin your journey of service learning.

1. **www.volunteermatch.org**
   This is a nonprofit organization that matches you to volunteer opportunities around the area where you live. Filter the search and save results for later. It is an easy website to compile a list of local opportunities posted by organizations around your local community.
2. **www.nationalservice.gov/serve**
   This is a great website that provides opportunities to serve with national organizations. Connect with professional helpers and receive funding for service projects. It is a powerful resource with the ability to offer help with various service projects.
3. **https://blog.prepscholar.com/129-examples-of-community-service-projects**
   This is a list of great ideas for local service projects that could be applied in almost any part of the country. The comprehensive list is broken down into specific ideas for doing service by working with groups of people or the environment, or connecting to organizations in your community.
4. **www.volunteer.gov**
   Volunteer.gov connects your classroom with opportunities to volunteer with federal agencies. It also allows you to search for long-term service opportunities. Stay at various locations for free—they provide the housing, you provide the workers!
5. **Your Local DSS or Town Council**
   Reach out to the local branches of government in your town and ask about challenges the community is currently facing. Connect with the people in charge of overseeing problem areas. Use local difficulties to tie content learning directly into students' backyards.

Reflection on Service

A page for you to reflect and write your own thoughts on the role of service in learning. Have a great idea or insight? Feel free to share at www.unlockingheroes.com

_____
_____
_____
_____
_____
_____
_____
_____
_____
_____
_____
_____
_____
_____
_____
_____
_____
_____
_____
_____
_____
_____
_____
_____
_____

Key Seven: Agency

Deuce Stith—Student
Artist, creative, magnificent, saxophonist
Hero

I love making people happy. Not only does it make me feel good, it makes others feel good. So when Mrs. Beachboard presented my class with the opportunity to work with Poet's Walk Assisted Living Facility to bring joy to residents, I jumped on the opportunity. I learned before going that a lot of the residents had dementia and Alzheimer's. We researched these diseases and ways we could help. I learned that by talking and spending time with senior citizens, I could help provide mental stimulation to combat their illnesses.

Since it was getting close to February, the director asked if we would want to do something for Valentine's day. The director told us that she had booked a band for the day. That's when it hit me: we could host a dance with middle schoolers and senior citizens! When I suggested the idea of a Valentine's dance to my class, a lot of kids got on board to volunteer.

Now, I am not the best at starting conversations, especially with strangers. But I thought, "What's the worst that could happen?" My desire to help gave me enough courage to know that I could talk to these new people despite how awkward it might be.

On February 14th, we headed to Poet's Walk after school. I'm not going to lie, when I walked in there, I felt scared and unwelcome. Doing something this different was like diving into a swimming pool and hoping to swim. But then I thought of my personal motto, "I can try to make some of these people happy."

I began going around and saying hello to everyone, but I was still really nervous. I felt like I had to do something to break the ice. So I went up to the front of the room and started dancing. I never knew that I could dance to bluegrass, mainly because I never listen to it. People started smiling, which made me smile. Then a nice lady came up and asked to dance with me. After about three minutes, we stopped and rested.

Everyone became more relaxed as we middle schoolers acted silly and danced with the residents. But after an hour, the bluegrass band had to leave. I started to wonder, "What were we going to do with the remaining time?" There was a lot of time left, so we had to come up with something. Then I remembered I had my saxophone. So I decided to go up there and keep the dance going by improvising. I was going to be the solution to this small problem. As soon as I got up there, I instantly got nervous. I had no idea what to play or say. But then I thought, "These people don't care what you play or what you say. This will keep things going and bring them some joy."

I began playing a random song that came from my head. I thought I sounded horrible, but then I saw a lot of smiles. Some of the residents began slowly slapping their knees to the rhythm I created. I felt accomplished. Not only did I face a fear, I made a lot of people happy. I didn't wait for Mrs. Beachboard to bring the problem to us; I fixed it. It was my event, and I took ownership of making it awesome. I'm still really proud of that.

It was a foggy Saturday morning when I (Cathleen) pulled up to Starbucks. When I entered the shop, a group of students and parents were waiting for me at a corner table. The students had asked me to be there for support as they worked on a video for the upcoming School Board budget meeting.

The group was in the midst of an intense conversation as I approached their table. Austin looked up, his black hair covering his glasses. "Mrs. Beachboard, how should we shoot this scene?" I looked down at their story map. The idea was to transition from the real world to an animation because they wanted to show their audience a world of possibilities.

"Well, what do you think your target audience would want?" I asked. Austin's eyebrows knitted together in frustration as I answered his question with a question.

Caroline chimed in. "We should make that whole scene animated because we want to show the community how our schools would benefit from this

Figure 7.1 Caroline Maier's art depicting her vision of a student landing on Mars. We always picture adults with ground breaking discoveries, but why not students?
Courtesy of Caroline Maier

budget increase. I've never done full people animation before, but Jada and I will figure it out." And just like that, they were off and working.

I met with that same group on three more Saturdays. They created a beautiful video, complete with animations, that highlighted how schools would benefit from more funding. One of the frames struck a chord with me so much that I want to share it with you, dear reader. In the animation, Jada and Caroline drew a student standing on Mars with a flag.

The picture is simple enough, but I'm blown away by what it represents. This group of real, normal students showed that with enough support, they envision a student (not an adult, a kid!) being the first person on Mars. Their video went on to show that this same kid might have the potential to cure cancer or create new, life-altering technologies. My students believed that all kids have limitless potential.

That belief got me thinking about agency. People have limitless potential tucked inside, but more often than not choose to settle. We settle for what's easy, safe, or normal. I've heard many teachers say, "These students aren't living up to their potential." But if even adults tend towards complacency, how do we get students to do something awesome?

We have to start small. I knew the students who asked me to meet them were using agency. They were working to solve a problem and they wanted my guidance, not leadership. It seemed like what student agency should always be. However, I'd heard the term used so many ways that I got lost in the definition. We need to understand what agency is in order to make it happen in our classrooms.

Agency 101

While preparing to write this chapter, I (Marynn) asked several colleagues to define or describe "student agency." Answers varied.

"Student agency? I've never heard of that."

"I think that's like the kids choosing what they want to do, right? Like on a project?"

"It's like taking the training wheels off a kid's bike—you give them independence, but also freedom to fail."

"Voice and choice! I know it has something to do with voice and choice, but I can't remember what."

My colleagues aren't the only ones who can't seem to reach a consensus on the meaning of "agency." There are different meanings in academic literature, as well! Cathleen guessed there might be as many as 15 accepted definitions of student agency in educational literature today. For the sake of simplicity, we're going to use the one found in "The Influence of Teaching Beyond Standardized Test Scores: Engagement, Mindsets, and Agency: A Study of 16,000 Sixth through Ninth Grade Classrooms." This is a study published in 2015 by The Achievement Gap Initiative at Harvard University. Despite the mouthful of a title, the study described student agency very simply. Here's what author Ronald Ferguson had to say:

> Agency is the capacity and propensity to take purposeful initiative—the opposite of helplessness.

Take a second and read that again. I don't know about you, but I find helplessness exhausting. Helpless students need endless attention and hand holding. Agency is the solution. When my students have "the capacity ... to take purposeful initiative," I'm free to guide the group without running myself ragged. I think of it as the difference between being a sheepdog and an alpha wolf. As a sheepdog, I'm worn out running circles to keep the sheep on track. As an alpha, I become the leader of a united pack. There aren't any helpless sheep to herd, only targets to chase and victories to win. Students with strong agency skills cease to be "sheeple"—instead, they become members of a wolf pack: strong, confident, and capable of working alone as well as in collaboration.

But where to begin? How do we begin instilling the skills that lead to students having agency within the confines of a traditional school day? I suggest "voice and choice." This means getting into the habit of asking students to share their ideas (voice) and giving them the ability to choose (choice) as often as possible. Let's consider how to implement voice and choice in a typical lesson model. Say your lesson plan involves students taking notes, reading a text, and then completing a worksheet. It's clean and concrete. As written, though, this lesson has no room for students to exercise agency. How can we improve it? Here are a few suggestions:

- **Ask students how they would prefer to take notes:** summarize the topic to be learned and then consider the pros and cons of two or three note-taking methods (limit choice options when first teaching agency to avoid overwhelming).
- **Allow students to choose how to read the text** (aloud or silently? with a partner or alone?) **or where to sit while reading.**
- **Explain the purpose of today's written work and collaborate with students to determine "look fors":**
  if you're looking for evidence of _____, what would "A" level or "meeting expectations" look like? Exceeding expectations? "C" level or "close but no banana?" Work briefly with student input to list descriptors of each quality level, then encourage learners to "choose your grade." Whatever level or score they've decided to aim for determines what to include in their work.

Voice and choice set the foundation for students to act and learn independently of the teacher. The goal is to move students away from helplessness. If you're thinking, "That sounds like it takes a lot of time," you're not wrong! At the beginning, showing children how to think through and pick the best option does take time. The payoff is enormous, though. Imagine a class full of kids fully on board with the work because they understand its purpose and had a hand in structuring it. Even when they're not *fully* on board, my students have stopped complaining, "why do we have to do this?" because they know. After all, they helped plan the lesson!

Cathleen and I have both seen voice and choice work to spark student agency—"the capacity and propensity to take purposeful initiative." If we want students to act independently, they have to feel that their opinions and ideas matter. Voice and choice are like training wheels. They give students safe practice with making decisions to affect their own learning. That safe practice, in turn, bolsters students' courage to strike out on their own. After all, like we described using the "glass of water" analogy in Chapter 4, if a student doesn't believe he can do something, he will never try. Voice and choice help build students' belief that they have the ability to learn without complete dependence on their instructors.

Scaffolding Agency

People start off as dependent creatures. When students become stuck, one of the first things they have been environmentally programmed to do is go to their caretakers for help. It's basic biology. The problem? If we help too much, those students will remain dependent. Learned helplessness will ensue. So where do we draw the line? How do we help while fostering independence? We can start simple with things like self-help flowcharts.

> **Tip for Teacher Heroes**
>
> Culturally, linguistically, and racially diverse students, as well as those labeled "special needs," often experience schooling that has been "dumbed down" or overly "modified." This leads to learned helplessness—students hear loudly and clearly the message that they can't do "hard" things without help. Being children, they believe it! Know that such students are equally capable of developing agency, but you'll have to push back against years of "you can't." It will probably take longer, maybe much longer, for these students to learn "you can." The end result is worth it!

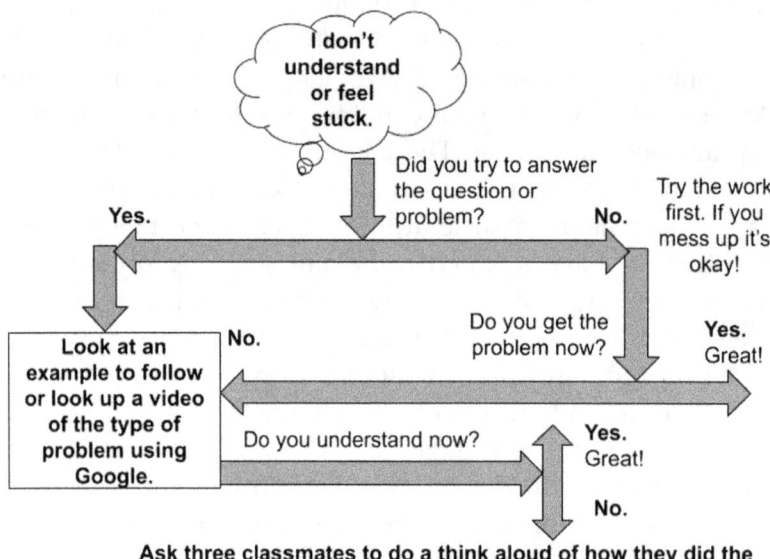

Figure 7.2 Example of a Self-Help Flowchart. These flowcharts provide scaffolding to autonomy as students begin the journey to agency.

Tracy Mulligan, a teacher from Texas, uses self-help flowcharts to give kids options for what to do when they become "stuck." For example, if a student becomes stuck logging into a computer, the problem-solving flowchart gives different ways to independently problem solve before coming to the teacher: make sure the computer is on, ask a friend, check the wifi signal, etc. Sometimes just showing students that they have the ability to problem solve can start them down the path to agency.

Self-help flowcharts and protocols like "ask three before me" are great ways to initiate agency with younger students. As students gain capacity, allow them a voice in the co-creation of flowcharts. This scaffolds students' ability to problem solve together and rely on their own thinking in the school environment. After a basic level of agency is introduced through classroom routines and procedures, students can begin using their agency skills while learning content.

Agency Cycle

If we want students to take charge of their learning, we've got to let them develop independence from their instructors. The role of the teacher when students are expanding agency is like being a friendly lifeguard at the pool. Lifeguards watch over the whole environment; they give instructions for new swimmers, sometimes swim next to reluctant ones, and dive in to help with big problems. Lifeguards are not strictly in control—they allow swimmers to freely roam and explore. Because, ultimately, how do you know if you can swim? If you can do it by yourself.

There are many ways to develop student agency with content. For example, you could try: project-based learning, service learning, genius hour, or student-created units—and that's only the beginning! The method isn't as important as the cycle that takes place when a student is growing agency. Through over a decade of working with students at all ability levels, it started to become apparent to me (Cathleen) that there are three phases students go through while developing agency. The order of the phases doesn't seem to matter much; I've seen kids start at each one of the three with equal degrees of success. What counts is that they eventually experience all three parts.

In order to know if a child has the means to "swim in the deep end," we teacher-lifeguards have to understand the parts of the agency cycle. We've got to know how to guide students during each phase. Remember, lifeguards don't usually stop folks from jumping in the pool: instead, they monitor constantly and offer feedback in the form of a whistle. In order to keep kids afloat while learning to use agency, the teacher's role is to monitor and provide feedback as students take on more independence.

Teacher feedback is what makes the student agency cycle work. As we learn new concepts, all of us naturally look to experts to see if we've achieved mastery. Then, based on what we see or hear the expert do, we adjust and try again. That is why feedback is critical. And again, the age of the expert doesn't matter much. In fact, as more students master concepts, they should contribute feedback on the agency cycle, too!

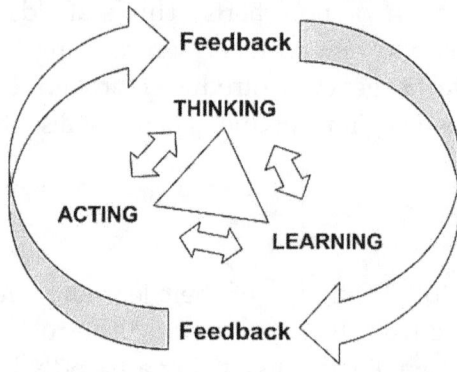

Figure 7.3 Teachers will need to adapt and contribute various types of feedback as students gain more agency in the classroom.

Let's take a look at the student agency cycle in action. I had a student named Kiki who wanted her class to learn more about World War II from the first-hand account of her grandfather. She knew our learning target was "understanding how setting impacts characters," and she saw this as a way to explore setting. She told me her grandfather was a boy when he and his family escaped Nazi Germany during the Holocaust. She asked if he could come visit us. Kiki started the agency cycle by *acting*.

When Kiki's grandfather came to visit, she and her classmates asked lots of questions. They looked at his artifacts from wartime. Everyone began *learning* new information about daily life in Europe during the war. The next day in class, we continued reading *The Diary of Anne Frank*. The kids started *thinking* about what they had learned. They asked questions about how daily patrols would have affected the characters and ended the lesson by writing reflections that summarized their thinking.

Kiki used her agency to accomplish something optional and awesome. Both Kiki and the students who worked together to make a video had high levels of agency because they'd already gone through the student agency cycle many times. After enough repetitions, they no longer needed my help.

But at the beginning, dear reader, there are things your students will need from you at every stage. Let's consider those now.

Agency: Thinking

In the thinking stage of the student agency cycle, students do the thinking. They ask questions, try out answers, and lean on one another for inspiration. The teacher guides this process with rich, meaty questions. Often, you'll also need to do a lot of cheerleading or individual coaching. One of our biggest jobs while students are thinking is to help get them unstuck.

Remember the lifeguard analogy? A student whose thinking has become stuck is like a swimmer who suddenly stops moving. You know what this looks like, of course: "zoning out," getting distracted, head down, or even panicky eyes glancing anywhere but at the work. What happens to a swimmer who stops moving? She may float for a while. That's when the lifeguard needs to check in and offer assistance. If you miss that critical intervention window, the next logical thing happens: your swimmer starts to sink.

So how does a teacher lifeguard offer help to a student whose thinking is stuck? This is where the analogy breaks down a bit. Unlike a lifeguard, we don't want to call undue attention. Making a scene or even calling loudly, "John, do you need help?" can set off a student's self-defense system. That sets him up for even more anxiety and stress. If brain science has anything to offer us as teachers, it's this: a brain in pain cannot learn. That's why the first step to helping a stuck thinker is to approach quietly with a smile and a calm tone of voice. "Hey, _____. What's up?" Even then, your student may not immediately confess that he's stuck. Be ready to follow up with a more specific question. "I see. You said _____. Can you tell me more about that?" No matter what, make it your mission to be calm and friendly. Only by sharing your sense of calm can you help a drowning swimmer regain his confidence in the water.

Once you've asked and answered often enough to know what's wrong, you can move into the coaching and cheerleading part of a stuck-thinking rescue. Repeat and rephrase for your student what he's said is wrong, or where he got stuck. Help him think of other ways to solve the problem, find the information, or approach the puzzle. Is there something he's missing? Is he frightened by something that seems too hard? Use your professional judgment to give him what he needs to get unstuck, and offer it with a smile and sincere encouragement. "I think you might be missing _____," you could say. "No big deal. I'll help you, and then you'll be back on the right track. You've got this!"

As guides on the side, thinking coaches, or metaphorical lifeguards, we've got to keep our focus on how students are thinking—as opposed to what. Conversation and constant check-ins are critical. Giving students time and space to think is *not* the same as setting a timer and sitting down at your desk to grade papers. After all, pro-level coaches don't sit and read the paper when their players are practicing! They're on the court, watching attentively, ready to jump in the moment a player shows signs of needing help. Educators call that help "feedback," but the process is the same. Watch. Listen. Stay involved, even when it's tempting to cool your heels. Make it your mission to know what's happening in students' minds, and then coach them on how to think even better.

Agency: Learning

In a classroom built around student agency, teachers and students can work as partners in the learning process. Cathleen and I (Marynn) both share our learning targets with all of our students. While Cathleen prefers open-ended questions, I tend towards checklists. The goal is the same, though: fostering students' ownership of the content. Again, there are countless ways to structure lessons and class time to share learning choices with students. Depending on the level you teach, you could provide paths to autonomous discovery such as webquests, stations, jigsaw mastery groups, curiosity quests, and the list goes on. The key is that learning must be available on demand for students to access as needed.

As students learn content through formative and summative assessments, the teacher's job is to provide constructive feedback so students can check their mastery, readjust, and keep learning. Here's a pro-tip: feedback sandwiches are your best friend! Perhaps you've heard that too much feedback is overwhelming, or that it's most effective just to emphasize one skill at a time. That's true. (And believe me, as a secondary English teacher, I feel the pain … how do you pick just one?) However, it's also true that people react best to feedback when it's given with encouragement. How to do that without being fake or floofy? Positivity sandwich. Here's how it works:

- Note one thing the student did well.
- Briefly highlight one thing that needs to change or improve; depending on difficulty, you may also include a suggestion about how to make the improvement.
- Wrap it up with one more specifically good observation.

This "sandwich" feedback gives students a base to grow from. In the learning stage, our job as teachers is to correct misconceptions and provide opportunities to relearn. Ideally, we want to do that before students begin using their knowledge to act! If you don't get to everyone or if a student fails while acting, though, no fear. As we'll explain in Chapter 10, failure can be the most powerful of learning tools.

Agency: Acting

Due to its nature, agency always involves students acting independently to own their learning. This is how students show what they know. Much like the lifeguard, we show our swimmers all the right strokes in the shallows. It's not until they go in the deep end (under our watchful eyes) that our learners know if they can swim. In the acting stage of the student agency cycle, students create a goal for their learning and act on it.

> **Tip for Teacher Heroes**
>
> If you're wondering, "How do I give second chances if the assignment is over?" you're not alone. Standards based or mastery-based grading help a lot with this. Since my school still uses very traditional grading, I've "hacked" my gradebook. So for one major assignment—say a project presentation—I'll use a rubric to score for several skills. "Timely completion" is only one skill. If needed, students are welcome to reattempt other skills later on to improve their score: I can stay after school to hear a second attempt at a speech, for example. The goal is for students to show me they've achieved mastery, no matter how long it takes.

Feedback in the acting phase comes in a variety of forms. Guided self-reflection, peer feedback, and teacher feedback are all important. During this phase, the teacher monitors all feedback. Our job at this point continues to be guiding students through questioning. We also provide further resources for exploration. Sometimes a student needs to be brought back to the learning stage if he is floundering in action. Note that "F" should not be a definitive grade if a student tries something once and fails. In the real world, people are given second chances and the ability to try again. Can't swim in the deep end today? You can try tomorrow. No one's going to banish you to the kiddy pool! Students will need to fluidly go through all three stages of agency multiple times as the need arises. Keep an eye out for times you can give struggling "swimmers" another chance to "dive in" when they're ready.

Empowering Students

Student agency in schools can be as big or as little as we want to make it. We can start small with questions like, "Could students be doing this instead of me?" Or we can go as big as having student summits where students meet and discuss issues that matter. The more power we give to students in the form of time, feedback, and resources, the less helpless they will become. Agency creates a shift in students' mentality. It shows kids that they really can affect positive changes in their own lives. With guidance, feedback, and the ability to try again, we can develop people who know they have the potential to change the world.

Unlocking Agency: Big Ideas

Locks:	Keys:
My students are doing great already. I don't need to teach them agency.	If students only know to go to their teacher with problems, they will develop dependence and helplessness. We need to teach kids to problem solve and be independent because they won't always have teachers to lean on.
My students are not ready for the freedom and responsibility of agency.	Agency should be scaffolded to meet the needs of your students. Try beginning with flowcharts. As students succeed, give them access to greater responsibilities.
I have way too many students to do agency. I can't give that much feedback!	There are multiple ways to give feedback: teacher feedback, peer to peer, student self-reflection. You don't have to do it all! Allow students to contribute to the feedback cycle.
I only have time to grade students' work once! I can't let them try again; it's not like they get second chances in the real world!	Students will not always master topics at the same time. In the real world, people are given second chances all the time. If I pay a bill late, for example, they don't cut off my access immediately. Let's model patience and allow students time to grow into content. Consider standards or mastery-based grading to help.

So what? Agency empowers students with the knowledge that they can direct their own learning and the course of their future.

Quick Resources for Agency

1. **Flowchart for Student Agency**
   https://drive.google.com/file/d/16DGOOlTXleHK9DVUHW2ebrd6RqrGPxLM/view?usp=sharing
   Agency flowcharts help students to learn to rely on themselves to solve problems. Flowcharts and protocols give children reliable, practical steps to follow instead of going straight to their teacher first. The link above is an example of an agency flowchart Tracy Mulligan uses with elementary students in Texas.

2. **Positive Self-Talk**
   www.ascd.org/publications/classroom_leadership/mar2001/Improving_Achievement_Through_Self-Talk.aspx
   Positive self-talk can help students stay motivated during agency. The link above provides tips for positive self-talk during the thinking stage of the agency cycle. Showing students how to use self-talk as a motivator gives them a valuable tool for when they need a boost.

3. **Feedback Tips and Timesavers**
   www.teachthought.com/pedagogy/20-ways-to-provide-effective-feedback-for-learning
   This website provides some great tips on a variety of ways to give quick feedback to students. It also gives information on best practices for responding to student work.

4. **Adding Voice and Choice**
   www.edutopia.org/blog/five-strategies-more-voice-choice-students-rebecca-alber
   This article describes five ways to add voice and choice to any classroom. The key is to take something you already are doing and look at it through the lens of voice and choice. A lot of the suggestions can be added on to practices you are already doing in your classroom.

Reflection on Agency

A page for you to reflect and write your own thoughts on student agency in the classroom. Have a great idea or insight? Feel free to share at www.unlockingheroes.com

Key Eight: Curiosity

Kyle Reviello—Student
Curious, sarcastic, observant, leader
Hero

My name is Kyle Reviello, and I try to view the world through as many different lenses as possible.

I have not always tried to do this. In fact, I only really started in November of my eighth-grade year. Before that, I was your typical middle school boy. I did what I needed to in class to get good marks, but I didn't really get into my learning. Then a question changed my life. One day I asked Mr. Woods, my World History teacher, why we measure time the way we do. At first he shrugged off my question. I kept asking, though, and the next thing I knew, we'd been arguing about time for three weeks! I started asking "why" about other things, too. Mr. Woods was happy to answer and debate with me. He encouraged me to dive into history and explore what our textbooks didn't teach.

One day, I found a thick novel sitting on my desk. It was *The Inferno* by Dante. I looked at Mr. Woods in confusion—why was this huge book, written by some guy who did not even have a last name, sitting on my desk? Mr. Woods looked at me and said, "Trust me, Kyle. Read this book. Read this book and ask questions." Of course, I was still a shallow eighth-grade boy. The book sat in my backpack for a month. Then one day, while waiting for a basketball game, I finally started reading. I got lost in *The Inferno* immediately. What fascinated me was that some of the people that our society most respects and sees as heroes were in hell! Homer, Socrates, Aristotle,

Julius Caesar, Frederick II, and Alexander the Great are all in hell in *The Inferno*. I started to realize that sometimes the world isn't what it seems. And though I didn't notice it at the time, reading *The Inferno* started to transform me.

After discussing Dante with Mr. Woods, he gave me *The Prince* by Machiavelli. He said that if I read and really absorbed it, I'd understand what makes people act like they do. The part I found weird was that *The Prince* is about ruling by fear. Machiavelli wrote about how the end justifies the steps taken to get there. How could this relate to how middle schoolers acted? But it did. After reading *The Prince* and then paying attention to how people interacted, I began to see that even regular people justify their actions by what they're trying to accomplish. Once again, my shallow eighth-grader self had another part of his brain kickstarted into action.

Finally, Mr. Woods gave me *The Book of Five Rings* by Miyamoto Musashi. In it, I learned how to train your mind and body to kill and dominate your opponent. But by reading between the lines, I also found out a lot about how warriors think and what it takes to be a good leader.

Mr. Woods took a chance on me. He encouraged me to ask questions and pushed me to be curious about everything in life, especially hard things like classic texts from history. That expanded my mind. It taught me to explore the world on every level I possibly can. One of the benefits I've gained being curious is simply learning about so many topics. Another benefit is that I'm never bored! Even in waiting rooms, I can occupy myself without technology. It's fun to look around and try to figure out what's brought each person to the office that day. Being curious about my surroundings and always trying to understand "why" drive my learning now. It's given me an edge—one I can keep for the rest of my life.

Students enter my (Cathleen's) classroom after lunch and stare in amazement as I tell them we will be researching the Pacific Northwest tree octopus. I bring up a website that gives scientific information on this endangered species. The kids nod as I read statistics about how many of these poor creatures are left in the wild. I show videos and picture after picture of this precious, endangered species. I even show the kids a link to donate to the cause. Then, a few minutes before the end of class, I inform everyone that the website is fake. Their eyes begin to twitch, and their faces scrunch together.

A boy in the back raises his hand. "How could you present information to us that isn't real?"

"I didn't make the webpage," I explain. "All I did was read and show it to you. Out in the world, it's up to you to determine what's real from fake. The only way to do it is to stay curious."

According to a report by Domo.com, "Over 2.5 quintillion bytes of data are created every single day, and it's only going to grow from there. In 2020, it's estimated that 1.7MB of data will be created every second for every person on earth." Our students have a wealth of information at their fingertips. Within seconds of a new discovery, students can have access to all of the related data anyone has ever gathered on the subject. The problem? With massive amounts of data, there can be miscommunications, misconceptions, and downright liars throwing falsehoods in the mix. For a little while, my students believed they needed to save the Pacific Northwest tree octopus. (Even though I told them it was fake, the next day a kid brought $20 dollars for the cause!) Knowledge is how we determine what's true. But how do we continue adding to what we know? The only way, dear reader, is to stay curious.

Teach Kids to Question

Skepticism has been given a bad rap. When someone questions information, people tend to get defensive. Why? Often, folks take offense that you are questioning their understanding. However, knowledge changes. In my own lifetime, Pluto was a planet and then got demoted to a dwarf planet. Currently, there are rumblings in the international space community that Pluto may be reinstated back to full planetary status. Helping students question information can help them develop a healthy skepticism. For example, recently I was excited to tell Marynn about a self-help book I was reading. Her initial response was, "What makes that guy an expert?"

I could have taken offense at the question, but it was a healthy dose of skepticism. In a world where anyone can publish a book, we need to seek information and proof of reliability. Students, too, need to be taught how to question and how to explore the world around them.

In my (Marynn's) ninth-grade English classroom, we spend quite a lot of time on the basics of asking good questions. "What are the words you can use to ask questions, again?" My students are fairly adept at listing *who, what, when, where, why,* and *how*. Putting a memorized list of question words into action by writing or asking questions, though—that takes practice. So we practice! Anything can be a teachable moment if you let it. Here are a few ideas to get you started:

- **The Bag Game:** bring in a bag of loosely (or not so loosely) related items. Students ask questions to figure out what each item is, how they relate to one another, or what kind of person might own this bag.

- **Wonder Walk:** grab some sticky notes plus writing utensils and take a walk. Where you go doesn't matter, although my students love doing this activity outside. The point is to practice asking questions. Challenge one another to write a certain number of questions on sticky notes before returning to the classroom. Then, see how many you can answer.
- **Get to Know You Interviews:** though a great community builder at the beginning of the year, this activity has so many possible variations that you can go back to it again and again. Begin by showing students a model of what you'd like for them to find out or create: a basic bio, listicle, "recipe card" detailing how to "make" a person/place/thing, etc. Give an example. Then, work together as a class to brainstorm effective, useful questions. Finally, pair students up and let them begin interviewing. This activity is most powerful when combined with a bit of self-reflection at the end. What questions worked best? Why? When being interviewed, what made you think too hard? Not enough? Just right?

I find that this kind of creative question asking helps build students up to being ready to investigate the things I really want them to explore: our curriculum! Once they've practiced with low-stakes activities, students can begin asking questions about content. Again, it's best to start easy. Take something small like a sample, article, or problem set, and encourage students to ask questions about it. Make it a game by trying to ask the most or the toughest questions. ("Stump the teacher" is a perennial favorite.) Then begin to transition into modeling and answering questions that lead to building knowledge. Consider sharing Bloom's taxonomy or Costa's levels of questioning. For the most part, my students respond very well to concrete structures that guide questioning the way these models do. It's also fun to see them puzzle over the differences between "level two" and "level three" questions.

A note of caution, though: most of the children we teach are still very concrete thinkers. Some may find it distressing to ask too many questions, while others will revel in their new-found power to question "the man." I've had more than a few upset by the realization that there might be more than one "right" answer. Be kind when this happens. Remember, the world is a big, frightening place! Children's brains are designed to protect them by classifying things solidly as safe or not, good or bad. I find it best simply to explain that when things have more than one right answer, it's ok not to know all of them at once. The idea is just to stay open to the fact that you'll learn something new tomorrow.

> **Tip for Teacher Heroes**
>
> Teach etiquette for question asking. Depending on the age of your students, you may want to host a discussion about what it means to be polite or respectful. Use the ideas of the group to establish norms *before* opening the floor to free-fire questions. I find it particularly useful to have "open" and "closed" times for question asking. For times that don't require that much structure, a simple, "I see that hand, and I'll be with you in just a moment" may suffice.

Explore

Speaking of learning something new: have you heard of makerspaces? It's likely that you have. The maker movement is big and getting bigger, at least at the time of this writing. So here's a better question: do you know what makerspaces/genius labs/tinker spots are *for*?

I didn't. In fact, I only "figured them out," so to speak, while wandering around an exhibition hall at ISTE—that's the International Society for Technology in Education's annual conference. Let me paint you a word picture. I was standing about an arm's length away from a broad, black table. The table was littered with bits and bobs. I saw cardboard squares, copper wiring, snaps like the ones on blue jeans, buttons, glue, paper clips, and more. Surrounding the table was a gaggle of children wearing "Ask Me!" badges on lanyards, as well as a jumble of adults. Everyone was busy building and reaching over one another. "Excuse me," I finally said to the lady standing nearest to me. "What are you all making?"

"Oh, I haven't the faintest idea!" she grinned. "Isn't it marvellous?"

I gaped. "You ... you're not making anything?"

"No, no, I'm making something," she said confidently as she turned back to her handiwork. "I think it may be a cricket or something like that. We just learned how a circuit works in my last session, and I want to see if I can get one of those in here." And with that, she was off and "making" again. The story was the same all around the table. Some participants had little printed paper "maps" that reminded me of origami instruction pages. Most were simply fiddling, seeing what happened when they put *this* with *that*. They were, for lack of a better term, playing.

As it turns out, that's really all a makerspace is—it's a structured place with odds and ends, and it's designed for play. As you know, play is the brain's most natural form of exploration. "Why are you kids up in the barn loft?" many an anxious farmer has asked. You know the response. "We were just playing!" When we play, we explore. Explorers are learners. Ergo, the more we can help our students play, the more they will explore and learn. But here's the trick: for school, we teachers have to find ways to let children play, make, and explore with our content.

For me, that means occasionally running "writing makerspaces," as inspired by my friend Betsy Potash of the *Spark Creativity* podcast. I have boxes of craft supplies that parents have donated over the years. We pull those out for projects, of course, but also for curiosity boosters: how can you show me what the theme in this story looks like using recyclable materials? What can you use to represent the water cycle? Whose actions from history can you best demonstrate using only the materials on this table?

Here's some good news, reader. When students are playing and exploring, you get to, as well. Leading by example applies in play as well as work. So, start playing!

Value and Reward Curiosity

One of the greatest ways we can foster curiosity in the classroom is to show we value it. At the start of the school year, I (Cathleen) encourage students to start a "spark" journal. When they see something that sparks their thoughts or emotions, I encourage them to draw, write, or take a picture of it and bring it to class. Once weekly, I ask students to share things that "sparked" them. This has generated incredible, wide-ranging discussions. By taking time to allow kids to be inspired, we show how much we value their curiosity.

Another valuable way to foster curiosity is to encourage students to show and tell. *This is not just for elementary school!* For the first quarter of the year, I have my eighth-grade students bring in things they enjoy learning or staying curious about. This small activity allows students to share their passions. It also sparks other students to ask new questions about things they've often never seen before. It's a great way to help students build rapport in their community of learners, as well.

Sometimes pairing students who are more curious with ones who are less so can have the same effect. Curiosity is usually contagious. Having students work in groups to generate questions takes advantage of the best aspects of "groupthink," and it's often less intimidating for students who may freeze up while working alone. (Be sensitive, though, to the needs of children who work best solo.) This helps show students that collaborating with other people is valuable when cultivating curiosity.

One more way to develop curiosity in the classroom is to reward questioning. I have a bulletin board in my classroom for students to "park" questions with sticky notes. At the end of the week, I read all the questions aloud and have the class vote on the top three. These are questions that approach content differently, inspire more learning, or require reexamination to answer. I give the top three question askers a pass for 10 minutes of unstructured free time to explore anything they're curious about. Curiosity is rewarded with time to foster even more knowledge building. This way, I also demonstrate that our class values curiosity and questioning more than simply knowing answers.

Sum It Up

Curiosity is one of the greatest things we can cultivate in students. By fostering curious minds, we push kids to engage with the world around them. Just by taking time to allow curiosity in our classrooms, we can save time presenting material. Why? With curiosity, kids are more energized and engaged. They learn more quickly because they're driven to fulfill a desire for new knowledge. Also, if you can put individual curiosity at the forefront of your lessons, knowledge will stick more easily because students will be actively seeking the content.

The best part about nurturing curiosity, though, is the excitement and life that come along with it. I allow my own children to play curiously all the time. Once my son CJ made popcorn before doing his chore of changing out light bulbs. As he cleaned the popcorn butter off his hands, he looked at the box of light bulbs and wondered aloud, "I wonder what would happen if I put these in the microwave?"

I quickly Google searched "light bulbs in microwave" and found that, with a little bit of water in a cup, a microwaved light bulb would light up. Thus assured, I told CJ that we were going to test his question. "Seriously?" he asked. Timidly, CJ put the lightbulb in a mug containing a bit of water. He shut the door and set a timer for 45 seconds. As soon as the microwave started up, CJ's face transformed. He screamed, "It lit up!" and sprinted off to get all of his siblings. Several demonstrations later, I began to put everything away. CJ disappeared. I found him on the family computer, reading up on electricity and microwaves.

By taking the time to kindle curiosity, we can inspire a renaissance of excitement for learning. There's nothing better than seeing a spark in kids' eyes as they rush off to learn all the secrets the world holds.

Unlocking Curiosity: Big Ideas

Locks:	Keys:
I already ask my students lots of questions to create curiosity.	Curiosity is more powerful when it comes from students themselves. Teach students how to ask higher-level questions and allow them time to practice.
I'm more worried about mastery than inquiry.	Real inquiry motivates mastery. When kids explore content and find things they want to know, mastery follows.
Free time for play is not learning.	Play is how children learn to make sense of the world around them. Play also makes learning more enjoyable for people of all ages. When students play, they begin to discover passions and insights about the world around them. Our job is to guide those discoveries towards a useful purpose.
I don't see the point in a makerspace. It's just a bunch of junk taking up space in the classroom.	Hands-on manipulatives allow kids to figure out abstract concepts using physical objects. Makerspaces simply take that concept one step further; rather than giving kids pre-made manipulatives, stimulate their curiosity by asking, "what can you make with *this*?"

So what? Curiosity is the spark that will keep students learning long after their final class has ended.

Quick Resources for Developing Curiosity

1. **Spark Journal**
   Give students a way to track and record their curiosity. This could be a physical journal, a folder in Google, a blog, a photo reel, and so on. The key is to get students capturing their moments of curiosity to share with others. My young daughter pastes pictures, flowers, seeds, and random things in her journal and loves to research the things she finds. This works for all grade levels and really breathes passion back into the classroom.
2. **Question Wall**
   Create a space in your classroom for students to post questions. Only questions should be visible, although you'll want to be able to

match questions to writers at the end of the week. One way to do this is to write questions on the front of sticky notes and names on the back. Giving a physical space for student questions shows that your classroom culture values inquiry. Plus, this is a great way for shy or quiet students to add to class discussions.

3. **Makerspace or Tinkerspace**
   www.edutopia.org/blog/designing-a-school-makerspace-jennifer-cooper
   A makerspace or tinkerspace is adaptable to teachers and environment. To create one, collect resources or things for students to use in a space set aside for making. You can also have a "pop-up" makerspace, like Marynn does in her classroom. I send letters inviting parents to donate unwanted objects. For bigger items, try donorschoose.org. You can design the space to suit your classroom and needs.

4. **Share Questions**
   A quick way to share curiosity is inquiry circles. Have students bring spark journals or something that makes them curious. Set students up in two circles, one facing in and one facing out. Students get one minute to share something that made them curious with the person they're standing or sitting across from. After about 60 seconds, trade roles. Then, have one or both circles rotate for new partners. Whether you use this method or more traditional show and tell, give students time to share things they're curious about. This builds rapport and ignites a passion for learning more.

Reflection on Curiosity

A page for you to reflect and write your own thoughts on using curiosity in the classroom. Have a great idea or insight? Feel free to share at www.unlockingheroes.com

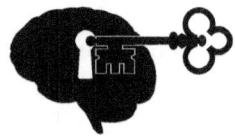

Key Nine: Innovation

Brandon Turman—Student
Charming, fun, quizzical, visionary
Hero

Some time in middle school, I realized that I think a little differently from other people. Any time we were given a project, I started thinking, "What would make this special? What would make it stand out? What will I be remembered for?" And then it just snowballed from there. Like when I was in Mrs. Dause's class, we did the Odyssey project. I wore a Roman centurion costume and presented about military strategies from ancient civilizations. The thing was, nobody expected it. Over the years I think everyone's just been like, ok, he's different.

Thinking that way, like I'm looking back on a good life, helps me take risks. When the risks don't work, I can learn from them. I want to be remembered as someone who always went above and beyond. I want to inspire people. So I just keep learning through mistakes. I go back again, figure out the right steps to take, and keep doing things differently until I get it right.

For example, with my passion project, I had to switch my goal a couple of times. Even though it was still the same subject, I had to change the methodology. When I started doing the passion project, I didn't know how to solve a Rubik's cube. I wanted to be able to solve a three by three cube in under a minute. I was aiming for world record level! But then I realized it wasn't going to happen in a month or two or three. It was going to take at least a year, so

I couldn't do it. But I did learn! I tried bumping my goal down a couple notches. The new goal was solving the cube in two minutes. I didn't give up.

I had to innovate during my passion project because I took on something that was actually impossible in the time frame. That was when I had to use divergent thinking. I had to find a way to move forward even though I felt stuck. I found out the way I was solving the cube needed to be different. I was using a beginner way, and I needed to learn the more advanced way of solving it. Even that didn't quite work for me, so I did more research. I went above and beyond. I started printing things out, working on it during my free time. Eventually, I came up with a solve that worked better for me. On presentation day, I was able to solve the cube in front of everyone—in less than two minutes!

Overall, my vision is if I can show you something new, if I can get you excited or interested by giving you a new experience, it might be enough to kind of shake you up a little bit. Help you think more about this whole universe of stuff that you haven't experienced yet. Sometimes I do get made fun of. Any time someone says, "Look, you're different," that's kind of a call out. In high school, I think you realize everyone's different, but people arrive there at varying speeds. So it's almost like by the time we graduate, hopefully everyone has kind of gotten the idea that the state of being different is normal. That when we step out and try new things, it doesn't hurt. It makes us stronger. That's why I want to keep innovating and doing "different" things: as a reminder that what happens in these walls is not everything in life.

I (Marynn) wasn't quite crying, but I sure wanted to. I'd been called down to the principal's office because a student's parents were upset with me … *again*. "Sir," I said after the latest angry email had been read aloud, "I don't understand it. I did all the right things. I emailed, text messaged, and sent home permission forms for this project. I offered alternate assessments, but they're still sending nastygrams. What gives?"

He looked me dead in the eye and said something I'm still pondering. "You're an innovator, Mrs. Dause," my principal said firmly. "And innovation always upsets *somebody*."

Eventually, the disgruntled parties were appeased. Peace was made. The project commenced smoothly. Still, I wondered; is innovation a bad thing?

What to Expect When They're Innovating

The answer, of course, is "no." Innovation is not bad. It's good! Innovation is how people solve problems. It's one of the most sought-after skills in new hires. Having an innovator's mindset can help you save money and live better; Sam Walton, founder of WalMart, was an incredible innovator.

Just like anything else, though, it's our job to teach children how to innovate. Want some good news? Innovation is relatively easy to teach. I think this is because humans are born problem solvers. That isn't to say that innovating is easy to *do*. It's hard! More than anything else in my life at school, innovation is one of the toughest, most rewarding parts of my job. The vast majority of my students have had similar experiences. "*Jeez*, this is hard!" eventually morphs into, "I am exhausted and never want to do this again," until finally we reach, "Ok, ok … that was actually kind of awesome." The key is having a solid process.

Creativity with Divergent Thinking

A great place to start is fostering creativity. All people are born with the power to create. By focusing on creativity, we allow development and holistic growth in our students. Creativity is an integral part of innovation. Making space for creativity helps students generate ideas.

One of the easiest ways to nurture creativity is to teach students divergent thinking. Dictionary.com defines divergent thinking as "thinking in an unusual and unstereotyped way, e.g. to generate several possible solutions to a problem." Practicing divergent thinking shows students that the more ideas we generate, the greater our chances of solving problems.

To start practicing divergent thinking, try the activity innovation specialist Tina Seelig presented in her TED talk, "The Little Risks You Can Take to Increase Your Luck." The purpose of this exercise is to show students that all ideas lead somewhere. First, have students write down two ideas for a new restaurant. The first one should be a "good" idea, like a five-star restaurant on a beach. The second should be a "bad" idea, like a restaurant that doesn't use dishes or utensils. Next, collect all of the ideas and have students form small groups. Ready for the twist? While students are forming small groups, throw away all the "good" ideas. Give each group a few "bad" ideas. Students should take a "bad" idea and, without taking away from the original concept, transform it into a great idea.

Here's an example. Remember the restaurant without dishes or utensils? One of my (Cathleen's) student groups turned that idea into a restaurant called "Catch!" When customers walked in, they'd see a sign that said, "No utensils, no dishes, only catching action!" The restaurant would be hibachi-style, and you'd have to try to catch your entire dinner. They'd have record-breaking challenges weekly to see who could catch the most food, and diners would only be charged for the food they caught. Ridiculous? Sure! The point is that this activity allows students to see value in all ideas. It sparks interest in divergent thinking.

The basis of divergent thinking is generating ideas. Students frequently want to think of just one idea and then blast off from there. By having kids focus on generating multiple possibilities, we cultivate students who can go beyond one solution per problem.

Strengthen Thought Processes

Students are bound to get stuck when they start using divergent thinking. There are four components we can use to strengthen their thought processes: fluency, flexibility, originality, and development.

> **Tip for Teacher Heroes**
>
> Have patience while kids practice this type of thinking. Most aren't usually challenged to think this way, and the learning curve may be steep. As always, be kind to your learners and yourself. The end is worth some frustration at the beginning!

Fluency means coming up with a lot of ideas. To build fluency, give kids a set time and a minimum number of ideas to generate. The time frame should allow students to think and even walk away from the problem for a while. If students freeze up while developing fluency, let them walk away from the problem and do something unrelated. Drawing pictures, building with Lego, and playing in a makerspace are all good ways to "rejuice" a tired brain. I've often seen students get inspired by two minutes of drawing and come back ready to tackle the problem.

Flexibility means finding connections between unrelated things. For example, I once had a student who was struggling to explain "symbolism." I knew this boy loved whittling, so I asked him to explain wood carving. He said, "When you start with the wood, it can be anything and represent anything. But as you narrow the wood, you make the object more concrete, like a bear. The wood isn't a bear when you begin, but it takes on the animal's features as you go. That's how you get to the carving you want." With that, we were able to begin a class discussion about how authors "whittle" meanings out of different parts of their stories. This new perspective helped everyone grasp the concept better. It also reminded me of the importance of finding connections between academic concepts and students' real lives. How could you encourage your students to practice flexible thinking with your content? Could a Math equation be represented with breakfast foods? What items in a toy box might connect with your social studies or history lesson? The possibilities, of course, are as boundless as teachers' and students' ability to think flexibly! Flexible-thinking exercises like, "What is it?"—a game where you pull items out of a bag and have students suggest unintended uses or names for each thing—entertain and sharpen thinking processes at the same time.

Originality, our third supportive process for divergent thinking, is easiest to practice with friends or classmates. Here's one practice activity you might use: when students are developing ideas for an upcoming project or to solve a problem, have them list three ideas they think everyone else will also come up with. Then the challenge is to avoid those three "everybody" ideas. Instead, try to create something that no one is likely to think of. This activity celebrates individuality and the power of original thinking.

The last divergent thinking process is *development*. This means helping students visualize how they form and make ideas actionable in the first place. One way to do that is to take a random concept and brainstorm how it might work. Sometimes just practicing planning how to move an idea from concept to reality helps students problem solve. This exercise also works well with traditional scaffolding: you know, "I do, we do, you do." Just make sure not to take too long! Once students have an idea or two they can believe in, it's easier for them to do further development using design thinking.

Teach a Process

Laura McClure, a blogger for TED-Ed, calls "design thinking" the "innovation cycle." I (Marynn) learned to call it "solution fluency." Students told me, "This is basically the scientific method, just applied to projects and stuff." Whatever you call it, the core concept is the same: in order to quickly and creatively find solutions, you've got to have a process. Following a process makes big, scary problems more manageable. Children thrive in structured environments, and brains in pain can't learn, so teaching a process for innovating covers a lot of bases at once! More than that, when you teach a system for problem solving, you're imparting a life skill.

This is how students transform into co-collaborators. It's not by giving them a project worksheet or recipe. In fact, I almost never do that any more.

In all of my classes, I begin by teaching the design process. I show students how I design lesson plans and assessments, and I begin teaching them how to solve their own problems. By the middle of the year, I no longer assign static work. Instead, I'll take time at a class meeting once a month to pitch the next set of standards and skills we need to master. I outline some ways we could pursue the new goals, and then students help me brainstorm our next unit of study. We write notes on the board for about 15 minutes. At the end of our planning discussion, I take a picture of students' ideas so I can type them up later. The next week, we review and revise the typed plan. Then we use the same process for summative and culminating assessments. Co-planning with students is a major way I share power in my classroom. It builds engagement through student ownership. But we couldn't do any of it if we didn't have a system to follow.

Tip for Teacher Heroes

If a process isn't working for your students, collaborate and change it. We must always be attuned to the needs of *these* kids in *this* classroom *today*. Adjust and improvise as needed to make processes fit the needs of learners.

Consider the six Ds of solution fluency. This is the model I learned from a Global Digital Citizen Foundation speaker several years ago. Although the "d" words can get a bit confusing, it was the first time anyone ever sat me down to show me, look, there's a way to do this. You don't have to reinvent solutions every time problems arise—you can have a system. I was mind-boggled. The next day, I told my students we were going to learn to use solution fluency together. Two weeks later, I excitedly mimed for them how my husband and I had used the six Ds while fixing a broken toilet. The six Ds solution fluency model is this:

- Define = figure out what the problem/challenge is. Define its parameters.
- Discover = find out everything you can about the problem. (Most folks call this research.)
- Dream = imagine the most perfect solution. Or three! Dream big.

- Design = make a plan.
- Deliver = execute the plan. Regroup, reinvent, adapt, and improvise when necessary. Reach your goal.
- Debrief = review what worked, what didn't, and what you could do differently next time.

There are other systems, as well. Cathleen taught me a super simple one recently: plan, prepare, act, reflect. Laura McClure wrote about another system with eight steps in a TED-Ed blog post titled, "How Educators can Apply Innovation Methodology in Everyday Projects."

No matter what system you use, remember this: children thrive when given structures to channel their ideas. Kids are incredible powerhouses of creative, divergent, innovative thinking, but they need guidance. By teaching and using a system for creative problem solving, you give students a means to unlock their potential.

Form Teams

One of the biggest untapped tools for innovation is teamwork. Yes, teachers often form student groups. Unfortunately, we rarely form teams. What's the difference? There are many. Here's an important one: groups work together to coordinate individual efforts. Teams work together because their members share a common vision or goal. This is one of the reasons Marynn and I (Cathleen) use service learning. Having a shared purpose like service pushes students to innovate. Purpose is power. Teamwork centered on a common goal is the difference between amazing, innovative work and "just another school project."

Collective knowledge is everywhere and powerful, but collective innovation is rare. In education, for example, we give awards for individual abilities and skills. How often do you see teamwork praised? In the grand scheme of things, one person innovating alone and getting the glory for it may be impressive, but it's still small. How much bigger and better it is when kids work together innovatively for a better tomorrow! My (Cathleen's) superintendent, David Jeck, ends all of his emails with this quote from Harry Truman: "It is amazing what you can accomplish if you do not care who gets the credit." Teamwork isn't about individuals—it's about utilizing everyone's abilities for a bigger purpose. Even while innovating, no one is good at everything. Still, everyone is good at something.

Four Types of Teamwork Abilities

Speaking of being good at something, have you ever attempted to break a Guinness world record? It's a lot tougher than you might expect. And as usual, it was my students' idea. Their service-oriented world record attempt taught me how important teamwork is. Not a single one of us could have broken the record alone. As I reflected on our experience, I realized that students' teamwork contributions fit into four categories: creators, planners, intervenors, and executors. Of course, people are incredibly capable beings. We all have the ability to fill any role. If we play to our strengths, though, amazing things happen. Put a player who is great at pitching on the mound, and your team may win the World Series! Just like if you give a person who is naturally a creator the ability to be in a creator position. Teamwork in the classroom is all about allowing students to explore their strengths and how they best contribute toward shared goals.

> **Tip for Teacher Heroes**
>
> Forming teams is *not* easy. It requires knowing students' personalities and providing a solid reason to become a team. Track what's not working, and keep adjusting until you've got it right.

Creators are defined by their ability to create possibilities. For example, my students took on a whole-class Genius Hour project with one goal: making a difference in the world. A group of 10, all creators, wondered, "Are there any local charities that benefit children?" They decided to work with A Little Heart, a nonprofit which provides stuffed animals to traumatized children. The creators dreamed up many ways to help. Together, they formed a vision for the project's end goal: breaking the Guinness world record for "the most soft toys hugged at once." Then, the creators reasoned, all of the soft toys could be donated to A Little Heart. Their vision became the framework everyone else followed. The creators inspired their teammates to go for the goal. I filled out an application for the class to attempt the record. Once we received approval from Guinness, the planners got to work.

Planners take over when it's time to figure out how to implement creators' visions. In our case, 10 new students brainstormed, planned, and wrote "to do" lists. The result was a shared document listing everything everyone must do, complete with due dates and back-up plans. When they hit a snag or got stumped, the planners went back to the creators for ideas. Then, the planners worked together to make the new ideas accessible for everyone. That's the power of planners; they are practical to the bone and turn dreams into action.

Interveners are frequently the "least favorite" members of their teams, but they're also one of the most critical. The best plans go into effect only after interveners have done their part because interveners look for holes. They find flaws in plans and have a gift for attention to detail. For example, one of the creators' ideas was to collect soft toys at our record-breaking attempt. However, the interveners pointed out, the folks who came out to help break the record might forget to bring stuffed animals. The interveners also noticed early on that to break the world record, we would need more people than the ones in my classes. Two students in particular were excellent at this job. They constantly challenged the group to make sure the plan was strong enough to work. It's worth cautioning, though, that interveners play an almost antagonistic role. Because they look for ways plans can fail, they frequently drive creators and planners crazy with "what if?" questions. Ultimately, though, they help tighten up ideas to create plans that work.

Lastly, executors make sure every part of the plan is done. Once our plan was solid, a group of four students made sure roles and responsibilities were fulfilled. As we got closer to the day of the record attempt, the executors volunteered to collect stuffed animals at community events. They distributed daily tasks to their classmates, and they handled problems. The executors were also responsible for bringing unexpected challenges back to the group, who began the innovation process all over again.

All of my students were talented at different parts of innovation. They needed each other to succeed. My takeaway was that, although I want my kids to be independent, they also needed to know that we're stronger and greater together. I also learned that we teachers are responsible for modeling all of the teamwork abilities. For example, I was both a creator and an executor for this effort—I planted the vision to "make a difference in the world," and then gave students access to others who helped achieve the dream. Still wondering how we fared? On April 27, 2019, my students successfully led the effort to break the previous record of 261 people hugging soft toys—we had 374. Due to a small timing issue we missed the deadline to be the official world record holders. Regardless, the kids changed the world and that is what truly matters.

Innovation Is a Survival Skill

So why is innovation important? Globalization, artificial intelligence, and competition are changing the face of jobs and society. A lot of previously paid work is already being outsourced or done by machines. It's said that we must prepare students for jobs that don't yet exist. In many cases, our kids will be the ones creating those new jobs. Innovation is key to students' survival because it allows them to create value from their ideas. By teaching students to innovate, we can help better ensure their futures will be bright.

Unlocking Innovation: Big Ideas

Locks:	Keys:
The activities and lesson plans I have work great. I don't need to add innovation.	If we don't change and allow students to innovate, we withhold a skill they'll need to survive as adults. For their sake, we need to help them learn how to look at problems differently. Plus, innovation often leads directly to higher engagement.
I just need my students to get the correct answer. I don't have time to teach divergent thinking.	Divergent thinking shows kids there are numerous possibilities and solutions to problems. It offers a way out if one solution isn't working, so it can help "get the right answer." More importantly, teaching divergent thinking helps students realize a whole world of possibility.
My students are already creative. I don't need to teach innovation, too.	Creativity and innovation are related, but without a process, many kids get stuck or "don't know what to do next." Teaching innovation gives kids a solid method for bringing their ideas to life.
I already put kids together in groups for projects. That teaches them teamwork.	Teamwork is developed over time and can only happen when students come together for a bigger purpose. Grades are great, but if kids are going to innovate, they need a better reason.

So what? Innovation gives students a path from "problem" to "solution."

Quick Resources for Innovation

1. **Divergent and Convergent Thinking**
   www.prodigygame.com/blog/convergent-divergent-thinking
   This blog features tools for practicing convergent and divergent thinking. There are also example scenarios that demonstrate how and why you might choose convergent instead of divergent thinking, and vice versa. These are easily adaptable to any classroom environment.

2. **Design Thinking Resources**
   www.teachthought.com/pedagogy/45-design-thinking-resources-for-educators
   There are a lot of ways to use design thinking in the classroom. This teaching website shares 45 resources for practicing, implementing, and using design thinking. There are also several quick activities to guide students through the design process using scaffolded instruction.

3. **Creative Warm-ups**
   http://arttech-metaphors.com/index.php/2016/06/21/more-ideas-with-creative-brain-warmups-and-icebreakers
   To help students practice thinking flexibly, provide opportunities for them to "think outside the box." The warm-ups on this site are meant to strengthen learners' creativity. The site also includes a collection of creative thinking activities to enhance everyday content lessons.

4. **Creating Teams**
   https://rework.withgoogle.com/guides/understanding-team-effectiveness/steps/identify-dynamics-of-effective-teams
   Google studied effective teams for two years. They came up with a list of what is needed to create an effective, innovative team. This website shares Google's discoveries and gives practical advice for building strong teams in any environment.

Reflection on Innovation

A page for you to reflect and write your own thoughts on student innovation in the classroom. Have a great idea or insight? Feel free to share at www.unlockingheroes.com

Key Ten: Failure

Hailey Lake—Student
Passionate, empathetic, creative, dreamer
Hero

I was tasked with reading the play *A Raisin in the Sun* for English class. Being an avid reader, I believed I was ready to take up the task and read it cover to cover. Unfortunately, that is not what happened. I had so much trouble focusing on the script that when I did finish, I barely remembered anything about the story. Usually I can pull through even when reading books I'm not interested in. Not this time.

While I was trying to read the play, I genuinely did not feel confident that I could do it. It was painful for me to sit and scan the pages. Then, after everyone was supposed to have finished reading, we had an assignment. We were supposed to write a short paper about which character was the most persuasive. I quickly found out that I had truly no clue what to write. I hadn't told my teacher, Mrs. Dause, how much trouble I'd had trying to read the play. Now I was in front of a blank screen with no ideas and no excuse. The feeling of failure welled up deep inside of me. I started crying. Frustration with myself and the book and the paper I was supposed to finish all just crashed down in a wave. I didn't know what to do. I could hardly think through all of the feelings.

My friend and Mrs. Dause were there, though. They helped me calm down and then suggested that I write a reflective piece about why the reading was so hard. That's the definition of failing forward. They helped me take a problem and solve it by learning from the failure. I learned more from this than I probably would have if I'd just done the essay as it was assigned.

My experience proves that when you fall or feel like you want to give up, failure is not the enemy. Failure is a teacher, challenging you to think around your problems. I understand this now, and I will not let the lesson go to waste. I'd advise you not to forget it, either!

I know this will not be the last time I am required to read a book that I cannot stand, nor is it the last time I will have to learn from failure. Henceforth, I have a plan for when I do encounter it. I will look at what is wrong, acknowledge how I got to that point, and find a way to turn it into a success.

To conclude, I will never ever like *A Raisin in the Sun*, nor do I ever intend to read it again. However, I do appreciate the valuable lessons it taught me. One, it is all right to bail on a book. Two, playwrights can be boring. And three, just because you fail, that doesn't mean you're a failure.

When I (Cathleen) was in elementary school I failed … a lot. I was diagnosed with dyslexia in first grade. I remember being frustrated when all of my classmates began reading easily. One day during a Math test, I bent my head and prayed. "Please," I thought, "Please give me this magic gift of reading. I need it for the word problems!" I promised to do anything in return for this super power of reading. Anything!

Of course, I failed the test. Months passed, and I fell further behind. Counselors put me in remedial reading classes. All I could think was that something must be *really* wrong with me. I found out failure has a way of beating you down. My grades slipped lower, and I started memorizing sight words just to get by. I knew my "reading" was a sham. Worse, my teachers knew it, too. Many blamed me. A well-meaning teacher asked when I was going to live up to my potential. Another one yelled, "Why won't you understand?"

Eventually I gave up. I believed that I had failed—reading would never be in my grasp. From then on, I saw no point in trying. What saved me? The only thing that ever does—a teacher.

In sixth grade, a lady I'd never met sat me down. We began in the usual way. "Well, Cathleen," she smiled. "I understand you have a big problem." I sighed and hunkered down, ready to endure another lecture. That's when she flipped the script. "But you've had other problems before, right?" Little by little, my new teacher drew out of me the story of how I'd learned to ride a bike. There had been a *lot* of bumps and scrapes. I'd persevered because

I had two good reasons: riding with my friends, and proving my "you'll never ride" siblings wrong. My new teacher worked with what I gave her. She built rapport, celebrating my victories and sympathizing with my hurts. Most of all, she taught me to reframe failure. "What did you learn from that?" she'd ask. "Why didn't it work? What did you do then?" That teacher's courageous combination of empathy, rapport, and perspective boosted me up. With her, all of my mistakes were interesting experiments. We were a team, constantly testing limits to find out what I could really do.

This is the power of our calling, reader. We teachers have the ability to touch the hearts of children and change them for the better. Failure is a touchy subject because so often it's humiliating and hopeless. But failure on its own is a great teacher. If we combine it with the guidance of caring educators, resilience and fearlessness will bloom in classrooms everywhere.

However, even the greatest educators can be stumped by failure. My teacher helped me learn to read so well that I ended up in honors classes. Once there, I noticed something odd; as the classes got harder, kids who never failed were terrified. My new classmates said things like:

"I need a 100 to get the highest GPA."

"I'm going for valedictorian and I have *never* gotten below an A in my life."

"My mom expects a 4.0 or I'm grounded."

I was not afraid of failure. Failure and I were old friends, and it wasn't scary. I just saw it as a starting point to move forward. My brand new peers, on the other hand, avoided failure like the plague. Perfection was their only option. Problems arose when they had to face something challenging, especially for the first time.

If you're the first one to do something, then you'll definitely be the first one to make mistakes or fail at it. Failure as a skill is underrated. It's a necessary element in creation. Used well, it's a checkpoint on the road to success and growth. When we teachers talk openly about failure with our students and their parents, we begin to remove the fear behind it. Just like my teacher did for me, we can help learners reframe failure as part of the process, rather than a dead end. We must do this to create an environment where curiosity overrides fear of failing. Imagine what students could do if they weren't afraid to try! They could tackle harder problems than ever before. They could walk boldly in new directions. They could even access realities only ever dreamed of before. It's possible! I'd even go so far as to say likely. But to get there, we need to help students learn how to fail.

Productive Failure

One of the reasons we saved this chapter for the end is that it's a bridge. Teaching kids how to achieve productive failure links the children of today to the heroes they will be in the future. Their world will constantly grow and change. Therefore, all students need to develop a high level of AQ, or adversity quotient. AQ has been described by educational futurists like Nancy Giordano as a quotient that precedes even IQ or EQ. You're probably already familiar with IQ, or intelligence quotient. EQ is similar—it stands for "emotional quotient," and we develop it in students by teaching social-emotional skills. If you've heard of growth mindset, grit, resilience, and "famous failures," then you're in the foothills of AQ territory. By empowering students to be aware of their AQ, failure and setbacks can become springboards to success.

Five Principles to Coach Productive Failure

In order to help kids fail productively and increase their AQ, it's best to start with failure itself. Coaches naturally deal with increasing AQ with players. The greatest coaches use failure as a tool to improve athletes' performance. Chris Cheshire, special education teacher and the National 14U Baseball Coach of the Year, is an expert at teaching productive failure.

> **Tip for Teacher Heroes**
>
> Coaching failure takes time. Often, kids need one-on-one attention to be able to move forward through hard experiences. My best trick for this is to keep an eye out for kids who are struggling, and coach them one at a time *as they need it*. This isn't the type of thing you need to or even should do as a whole class or in an orderly, "take your turn" way. Also, coaching through failure can happen via messages, emails, video recordings, and even sticky notes. Generally, though, face to face at the spur of the moment works best.

"We all have to deal with failure," Chris says.

In my career as a coach and special education teacher, I've had to address many tough moments of kids failing. These are never easy conversations to have, which is why while talking to a student, team, or player, I depend on these five principles:

1. **Empathy and Ownership**
   One of the best things we can do for any kid is to take the time before coaching to reflect on our own failures. I reflect on a time I went through it. How did I overcome? What did I need in that moment? How can I best help? By sharing stories and finding empathy, we can create a bond of commonality to pull kids from staying in the moment of letdown. It also shows kids how to take ownership. People tend to blame others for screw ups. When kids know how to take ownership, they gain control to create change.

2. **We**
   Failure is a dark and lonely place, especially to an adolescent mind. I will never let a player or student feel alone during failure. When I talk to them, the words "I," "me," "you," and "they" are out. The only acceptable word when trying to help someone overcome failure is "we." We solve this by, we will do this, we will try … "We" is more powerful to a kid than the actual success. It shows kids that they are not alone. It also models how teammates and classmates have the power to push each other past failure.

3. **Find Your Words**
   Anybody can talk, but not everyone can talk through failure. It's important to find the right words for the situation. The best way to get the most from a conversation is to use rapport to make what you're saying relatable to the player. Feedback on what the failure looked like from the outside can be the difference between the student accessing a solution or thinking you're criticizing them. Constructive feedback with the motivation that comes from a personal relationship yields the greatest success.

4. **Why Are We Here?**
   One failure or loss is small in the grand scheme of things. I remind kids to think about how many things they've already overcome. We talk a lot about how the *way* you do things is more important than the outcome. I'm not too worried about a single win or loss. It's much more valuable to think about *how*. How did success or failure happen? The very best question to ask is why? Why am I here? Why did I try to do this in the first place? Why am I willing to try again? When you put failure in its place in the bigger picture of life, it shrinks. It lets kids look at their failings and reflect without getting overwhelmed.

5. **Plan**
   Planning is the single most important piece of the puzzle. I built my entire coaching and teaching career around this proverb: "If you fail

to plan, you plan to fail." You cannot resolve failure for anyone without a plan. Know how to fix the problems. You have to begin with ideas for solutions. Ultimately it is up to the kids to take action, but my job is having plans that will lead to action.

Separating Knowledge from Performance

Speaking of plans, one that's been transformative in my (Marynn's) grading life is deciding to find out what kids know, rather than how well they can perform. It's a subtle distinction that's made a huge difference: kids may *know* content without succeeding at what I've asked them to do with it. I watch for disconnects like this, and I've got a plan for what to do when they happen.

> **Tip for Teacher Heroes**
>
> Remember, failure feels *bad*. It's said that "a brain in pain cannot learn," and few things hurt like messing up big! Kids react to it emotionally. You can expect curt answers, raised tempers, and every other sign of an emotional overload. Prepare for this by building a tool set of calm-downs. Learn about amygdala hijacks, self-soothing, and grounding techniques. Talk with your school's counselor for tips and tricks. Be ready to soothe the emotional response before diving into the logic of the situation.

Take Cora, for example. She took off typing furiously when I gave her class a writing assignment. It wasn't until sharing her work days later that Cora realized she'd written the wrong thing. Not only had she misunderstood the prompt, she hadn't followed the order of argument that I'd assigned. Cora's eyes glazed over as a peer pointed out *many* flaws in her writing. Her cheeks flushed. She started punching the bench she sat on. I practically ran to her side. "Whoa, there, champ. Breathe it out. In. Out. There you go. What's up?" Furiously, Cora gestured to her screen. She explained her mistake in broken gasps. She was enraged with herself for failing.

In past years, I may have shrugged it off. I could have told Cora I'd take some credit off her final score. Or perhaps had her stay late with me to rewrite the essay. I may have chided her lack of attention to detail. On a really bad day, I might even have rolled my eyes and told her to "just deal with it somehow." (And to any students I ever spoke to so harshly—please forgive me! Teachers learn from failing, too.) That was then. Now, I knew something Cora didn't. "Look at this," I said. "Look at this paragraph. It's beautiful! Your writing is solid. There's nothing wrong with what you've actually written."

"Except that it's *wrong*!" she wailed.

"Well," I returned, "It's not what I expected, that's for sure. But you know what? I'm scoring two things with this assignment, not just one. One is your ability to write, and you're killing that. You're a great writer. The other thing is how much you know about the argument structure we've been learning. And you understand that ok, right?"

Cora sniffed. "I mean, I guess."

"Ok," I smiled. "So here's what we do. You finish writing this essay. You've worked hard on it, and you're doing a good job of showing me how well you write. Tomorrow, let's sit down together and you can talk me through what you know about the argument structure."

At her confused glance, I continued. "It's called an oral assessment. I ask you questions and take notes on your answers. Then, I figure out how much you understand based on what you say. Sound fair?"

"Yeah," Cora said. The red was fading from her cheeks. "Yeah, ok. I can do that."

Do you see the difference, reader? Years ago, I may have been too frustrated to see what surely stands out to you. Cora misread my directions, yes. She didn't pay as much attention as I wanted her to, but that *wasn't what I was scoring*. She did know how to write, and she did know how to use the argument structure. (She scored 84% on her oral assessment.) She may have "failed" at the performance task I'd designed, but that didn't mean she was lacking knowledge.

How often does that happen to other students, I wonder? For that matter, how often did it happen to me? I recall many times in every grade when teachers' assignments didn't line up with the way I understood the material. Why build a model of a steamship when I saw *Huckleberry Finn* in color and tasted the flavors of its setting while I read? When studying physics, I grasped concepts when we experienced them kinesthetically. If someone could have helped me connect the physical sensations of centripetal force to the symbols used in equations, I might have understood them. Did that ever happen to you?

I know our time, attention, energy, and practically every other resource are finite. Teachers can't serve the individual needs of every single student in their classrooms—at least not within the traditional structure of the school day as it's run right now. But hold this in mind, if you will: what we know and what we successfully do don't always align. Whenever you can, share that grace with your students. Give do-overs. Give them to yourself, too! Failing at a task once doesn't always mean the knowledge is lacking. Look for it some other way, and you may find understanding hiding in plain sight.

Manage the Effects of Failure

All that said, I doubt failure is ever going to feel *good*. It probably wouldn't have so many benefits if it was as enjoyable as success. The point is simply to build understanding in students that we expect failure at the beginning of learning. It's a waystop on the road to understanding. To that end, we must mitigate "consequences." I'd feel awful if my girlfriends chewed me out for screwing up a baking recipe the first time I tried it. You probably would, too. Common sense tells us that students will feel betrayed if we ask them to try something new and then *wham*—smack them with an "F" when they mess up. If you already know this and score first attempts gently as "practice" or "learning opportunities," congratulations! If this idea is new, I congratulate you even more. That's learning!

It's worth discussing with students how and why you grade work the way you do. A community of learners can work together to set scoring expectations that make sense. "How many points should a first attempt count for?" you might ask. "What can I look for to know you're really trying? What do I need to give back to you to help you learn even more?" These conversations are easiest to have, in my experience, if you're using some version of mastery-based grading. Traditional gradebooks can be hacked to allow this kind of flexible scoring. The learning curve involved in talking through these issues with students is well worth the trouble at the front end. With a solid understanding of what you're looking for and why, students are freed to try, fail, and try again without fear of repercussions for bringing home poor grades.

Tip for Teacher Heroes

It's best to front-load expectations for families, guardians, and admin, as well. Be transparent about how and why you're trying to develop students' AQ. When people know what to expect going in, they tend to remain calm later on. Plus, we've found that many families whole-heartedly support teaching students to be resilient, especially when they're assured the lesson won't negatively impact their children's grades in the long run.

Keep in mind, too, the power of encouragement. My (Cathleen's) son had a civics teacher who understood the importance of a pick-me-up. Mr. Walker helped mitigate the effects of failure with encouraging notes written by parents and guardians. At the beginning of the year, he sent a letter home to all families asking for cheerful notes, postcards, collages, and the like. He also asked his students' former teachers to contribute. In this way, he made sure that every student had at least one encouragement letter. He used those pieces to help students rebound from stress, anxiety, and failures.

This simple trick reminded me that we are not the only ones who can help kids build their AQ. Instead, let's remind students of the village standing behind them: family, friends, staff, coaches, pen pals, etc. Regardless of students' failings, we can work together to help them be bold, determined, and brave. Encouragement says, "someone will be here to catch you when you fall."

Sharing Failure

When we fail, emotion often takes over. It becomes hard to think reasonably. Like Chris Cheshire says, failure feels isolating. That's why it's so important for both children and adults to reach out to friends and mentors. These outside observers have two important qualities: they're not emotionally tied to our failure, but they do care about us. When children talk through their mistakes with someone like this, they begin to calm. They can ask questions, process aloud, and hear new perspectives. After all, it's easier to stand up when someone gives you a hand. Recovering emotionally is similar. Failure summits in the classroom are a useful way to teach this resilience skill.

Failure summits originated in the field of engineering. The idea was for engineers to share what *didn't* work so their fellows could try new things that might. During a failure summit, students share their failed attempts from school, sports, or home. These can be recent failures that have already resolved or current setbacks that are still fresh.

Hosting a failure summit normalizes mistakes. It allows students to learn from each other and use failure as a springboard for new ideas. For example, I (Cathleen) had a student who struggled with public speaking. He memorably screwed up presenting a project in sixth grade. The memory hurt so much that he refused to participate in class seminars. During a failure summit, he spoke about his failure in sixth grade and how public speaking still scared him. Another student leaned forward. "I felt the same way," he said. This second student shared a grounding technique he used to tame his stress. It began a conversation with the whole class about grounding techniques and anxiety. It was powerful to see how sharing one failure led to a bunch of students gaining tools to manage stress and fear.

On the other hand, some students aren't comfortable talking openly with their peers, especially about things that hurt. Plus, we're not always surrounded by a loving community of supporters. What's a learner to do then?

In times when solitude is preferred or required, personal reflection is your best tool for looking back at failure. The easiest way to do this is to pose the following questions: what went well? What went poorly? Why? How can I do it better next time? Sometimes, though, even this isn't quite enough. For big hurts, teach students to "watch it like a movie."

"Watch it like a movie" is a technique I (Marynn) learned from a friend who was also a licensed clinical counselor. It's a type of guided visualization that helps you distance yourself from the "bad" or "fail." Once you know the format, it's pretty easy to do on your own. That makes it an excellent tool for introverted and shy students—they can use it subtly as needed.

Here's how it works: first, picture a small, black and white television screen sitting about two feet away from you. It might look like an antique TV set or maybe a security tape replay machine. Once you've got that firmly in mind, replay the "tape" of your moment of failure. Imagine watching it from a distance, in black and white, on that tiny screen, all the way from beginning to end. This part can be hard. Failure is painful. We don't like to think about it. So, if needed, spend some time just practicing rewatching the "film" forward and backward. Another powerful aspect of this exercise is that it's visual, not verbal. Encourage learners to simply see what happened in their mind's eye, without worrying too much about how to describe it. Finally, when you feel comfortable with your "replay," watch it all the way through one last time. Then, press "pause" and imagine you can talk to the main character (yourself) on the screen. Take a minute to tell him or her what happened after the moment of failure. Describe what happened the next day, and the day after that. Explain that even though what happened in the movie felt bad, you're still alive, and you're moving forward. Maybe even add something nice like, "You've got this," or "I still love you."

Though it may seem "mushy gushy," this private exercise is unparalleled for putting moments that feel bad in their place. Learning to reflect in this way helps students realize that failure isn't the end. It gives them a chance to practice useful self-talk, too. That way, the next time they fail, they've had some practice with being resilient and trying again more quickly.

Failure in Summary

Failure is everywhere. It makes life worth living! Think about video games, books, and foot races; people would stop playing video games if they were easy. Few adults enjoy reading books that are predictable. Winning a race would mean nothing if everyone else won, too. Students need to learn how to appreciate failure because we can't grow without risk.

Risk is the opposite of comfort. Being comfortable is often equivalent to being compliant. If kids only rarely face failure, they remain in their comfort zones. I, for one, don't want my students to be too comfortable or too compliant. All of us are trying to write awesome life stories—if there's no need for courage, how will we write life stories worth reading? We said at the beginning that we want kids to lead lives true to themselves. To do that, our students need to know how to fail like a hero.

Unlocking Failure: Big Ideas

Locks:	Keys:
I have too much other stuff to teach—I don't have time to talk about productive failure.	The content we teach is important. However, our kids will eventually struggle with failure. If they don't know how to deal with it, none of the rest of our content is going to matter much.
Failure is not acceptable. It should not be encouraged.	Failure is inevitable. By showing kids ways to turn problems into opportunities, we build their adaptability quotients so they can thrive in any situation.
I am not willing to share my own struggles and failures.	Appropriately sharing our own mistakes helps create the mindset that failure is just a part of growth. Opening up about times you've messed up humanizes you to your students; it lets them see that failure is a part of real learning.

So what? We will all face failure. Our reactions can be the difference between students' learning growing or slowing down.

Quick Resources for Learning from Failure

1. **Failure Pick-me-up**
   Send a message at the start of the year to parents, guardians, and other teachers in your school. Ask for encouragement letters for your students. Store these encouragement letters and use them when your students struggle. You can save them for difficult moments of behavior management, students having "down" days, or the hours before standardized testing. This little pick-me-up reminds students that they are not alone.

2. **Gallery or Individual Critiques**
   A great way to encourage productive failure is to have students critique their own work as well as each other's. This shows kids that messing up or making mistakes is part of the process for making their work better. It models how collaboration can help solve problems.

3. **Failure Summits**
   In a failure summit, students share all sorts of failures. One way to do this is to give students time to compose a short PowerPoint presentation. Preview and approve these presentations ahead of time. On the day of the summit, students take turn presenting to small groups that rotate around the room—I find that four or five groups work best. This allows students to have small conversations and gather lots of new ideas. Most importantly, it shows how sharing failure can push you forward.

Reflection on Failure

A page for you to reflect and write your own thoughts on using academic failure in the classroom. Have a great idea or insight? Feel free to share at www.unlockingheroes.com

Afterword: Hope

Why do we teachers spend hours trying to perfect what we do? It's because we know that, every day, we are teaching the future of the planet. We are daily difference makers, and we want that difference to be for good.

I (Cathleen) was once obsessed with becoming a perfect teacher. I never wanted to show weakness or doubt in front of my kids. It wasn't until they challenged me to lose weight that I finally learned the truth—students need to see me being imperfect. My kids learned so much from helping me improve! Perfection couldn't teach them, but the process of transformation could.

That's why our classrooms have to change yearly, if not every day. The people we serve are in process. It's important to help our students become the best version of themselves because the world needs them. It needs their ideas and their service. The future of our planet depends on each of our kids being authentically, positively *them*. We, dear reader, hold the keys not just to engagement but to empowerment. We can and should help our learners take control of their own lives for the purpose of doing good.

This book has given you keys to unlock the hero in each of your children. With you as a guide, they can write stories where it's ok to be transparent about brilliance and breakdowns. The biggest thing we want to leave you with is hope. There is hope for all of the heroic teachers taking this journey towards student empowerment. We believe in the amazing things you will do!

Sometimes, though, onlookers don't remember that Superman is also Clark Kent. Those on the outside forget that their strong, capable hero is also fragile. He is vulnerable as he tries to fit into the world. Marynn and I want to give you hope that in a world of heroic teachers, we are here for your Clark Kent side. We are here for you, dear reader. That's because one of the greatest things any of us can give one another is support and encouragement.

Self-doubt tends to loom when starting a new adventure. When Marynn and I first started working to empower our students, both of us felt like explorers in a brave new world. It was exciting but solitary, especially because we hadn't met each other yet. The journey won't be that way for you. We're here to help you find the way, and so is everyone else who has read, is reading, or some day will read this book. We'll move forward together as you give the best you can to the students in your care. Feel free to share this book. Join or build communities of empowerment. But most of all, write to us, chat with us, and email us. We are here. And, now, so are you.

For Product Safety Concerns and Information please contact our EU
representative GPSR@taylorandfrancis.com
Taylor & Francis Verlag GmbH, Kaufingerstraße 24, 80331 München, Germany

www.ingramcontent.com/pod-product-compliance
Lightning Source LLC
Chambersburg PA
CBHW080925300426
44115CB00018B/2942